Beyond Diversity and Intercultural Management

BEYOND DIVERSITY AND INTERCULTURAL MANAGEMENT

CHRISTOPHER ANNE ROBINSON-EASLEY

First published in 2014 by
PALGRAVE MACMILLAN®
in the United States—a division of St. Martin's Press LLC,
175 Fifth Avenue, New York, NY 10010.

Where this book is distributed in the UK, Europe and the rest of the world,
this is by Palgrave Macmillan, a division of Macmillan Publishers Limited,
registered in England, company number 785998, of Houndmills,
Basingstoke, Hampshire RG21 6XS.

Palgrave Macmillan is the global academic imprint of the above companies
and has companies and representatives throughout the world.

Palgrave® and Macmillan® are registered trademarks in the United States,
the United Kingdom, Europe and other countries.

ISBN: 978–1–137–40513–5

Library of Congress Cataloging-in-Publication Data

Robinson Easley, Christopher Anne.
    Beyond diversity and intercultural management / by Christopher
Anne Robinson-Easley.
        pages cm
    Includes bibliographical references and index.
    ISBN 978–1–137–40513–5 (hardback :alk. paper)
        1. Individuality. 2. Diversity in the workplace. 3. Organization.
    4. Personnel management. I. Title.

BF697.R593 2013
658.3008—dc23   2013042422

A catalogue record of the book is available from the British Library.

Design by Newgen Knowledge Works (P) Ltd., Chennai, India.

First edition: April 2014

Contents

PREFACE

Many recent events in our world caused me to expand how I posit the concept of difference and diversity even as I continued to write this book. When we look at difference from the lens of valuing and loving humanity, we can significantly move beyond the need to engage in the varying diversity and intercultural management strategies that over the years have made questionable difference on how we globally interact with one another. Valuing diversity, managing diversity, managing intercultural relations, and all the other references we attribute to evoking acceptance of one another in our global society cannot override a fundamental concept ... when we learn to value our humanity without process descriptors, we can work toward valuing one another simply from a lens of love. You see, "Love is the strongest force the world possesses, and yet it is the humblest imaginable," (Mahatma Gandhi).[1]

I initially began writing this book from the point where I began my journey with the concept of diversity—during my years in the corporate business sector. As a result, the primary focus of the book was to look at the concepts of diversity and intercultural management solely from the lens of workplace environments and at the global impact of that worldview. Yet, as I continued to write, many issues emerged in our global context that moved me to reconsider some of my original praxes.

I had the opportunity, over the course of a 20-plus years career in human resources and organization development, to witness how organizations handled difference from the early inception of implementing the vast array of civil rights laws, through a variety of diversity management strategies that incorporated interventions such as sensitivity and diversity training. During the latter part of my career I have taught, researched, published, and consulted in the areas of diversity and intercultural management. Yet, what plagues me each time I stand in front of my students and/or groups that I work with or consult to, is that I still feel a nagging doubt that little has changed since the very beginning of my diversity journey in the 1970s.

Recent global events have sensitized me to understand that if we are to change our world, we should view the concepts of difference and how people perceive and react to the injustices they see associated with difference from very different paradigmatic perspectives. Oftentimes, perceived injustices are not just ignited by reactions to the more acutely observable differences. Just as the concepts and constructs associated with diversity have expanded, so have people's responses to issues of how they view treatment toward them.

As I worked to finish this book during the summer of 2013, for several weeks I daily heard and/or read about people making the choice to voice, in huge numbers, their concerns with what they perceived to be varying acts of oppression on the part of their governments and other country entities.

Turkey, a country I grew to love very much, was in civil discord for the majority of the summer. While many will cite varying reasons as to why Turkey has and continues to undergo unrest, I have to rhetorically ask the question whether many of the issues that reside within the domains of this civil unrest are fueled by the different microcultures that reside within the country and the perception by many of their people that there is an inappropriate execution of domination and power by those in power.

As I traveled through Turkey in 2008 and 2010, I saw multiple influences informing the Turkish economy due to its geostrategic position. The fact that Turkey is primarily a Muslim country also influences and informs its perspective and approach on the effective management of its human capital. Yet, there are many microcultures that reside within this country for a variety of reasons, which means one cannot draw broad conclusions regarding the cultural context— you should do your research in order to effectively understand the issues people are addressing.

In today's global environment, where we are now working with many more sophisticated issues such as the geopolitical nature of this country that straddles both Europe and Asia, a valid question is whether or not answers to these looming questions should be framed within old and/or even prevailing paradigms and resulting strategies.

I think not, and this may be the challenge facing the Turkish government and its people.

Within weeks of Turkey's civil ongoing unrest, thousands of people took to the streets in Brazil to protest over issues that some may simply have relegated to socioeconomics—but again the same rhetorical, yet prevalent question prevailed. For years, poverty has been a serious issue in Brazil. When I was researching youth gangs on an international level, I was appalled by the stories of poverty, domestic violence, and abandonment that still confronted many Brazilian children sent to the streets to make money for family support, often being recruited as foot soldiers for gangs, placing these children at heightened risk for AIDS and acts of violence (Jeffery, 1993; Economist, 1993).

I cannot help but again rhetorically ask if the domains of diversity are being inadvertently expanded by society due to the times in which we live—times where people are less tolerant of actions imposed by the varying "systems." Are people uprising because they believe their humanity, framed by many microcultural differences, is being challenged?

Following the civil unrest in Brazil, just a few days later, people in Egypt began engaging in protests of the one-year-old government. The gamut of issues each country is addressing ranges from concerns that their varying civil and religious freedoms are being infringed upon to issues that the governments are failing to meet the economic needs of the people.

And, days after I emailed this manuscript to the editor for review, the United States was torn over the Trayvon Martin verdict. In August 2013, people in the United States noted and commemorated the fiftieth anniversary of Rev. Dr. Martin Luther King's "I have a dream speech" and the March on Washington. Yet, despite the passing of 50 years, far too many people across multiple venues and forums are boldly stating that this country, my country—the United States of America—has made insufficient progress with how we treat people of color, citing multiple acts of injustice that continue to prevail—even in the midst of our having an African American president.

The issues are overwhelming and the concerns run deep. Equally disturbing, there is an element of unrest that closely resembles the early 60s. I will not begin to espouse an understanding of the issues as they pertain to the international arena, simply because I do not live in these countries and I have only spent time in one—Turkey. Yet, I have lived all of my life in the United States and have an acute awareness of why people from multiple walks of life and race are still very concerned about equality.

We are emerging into different times. I also suggest that the emergence of these times will require our diversity conversations to expand. Equally important, our actions toward ameliorating injustices that are based upon differences will be held to higher standards.

Many people across the globe are angry about the failure to see and, more importantly, experience change. The negativity that we are bombarded with in concert with more salient issues that contribute to the destabilization of people who live with challenges to their humanity and diversities, can and does impact how people internalize self-worth and vision their ability to collectively question that which is placed in front of them as "truth." I have seen these issues, having worked with challenged communities within the United States. Yet, at some point in time even the most subjugated people will wake up! Ironically, Paulo Friere wrote about the awakening of the masses in the 1970s as he worked with challenged communities in Brazil. And here we are—40-plus years later having similar dialogues.

A concept that will be repeated in several places within this book is that our knowledge of social phenomena is fundamentally shaped by the *subjective* worldviews through which we perceive events (Tenkasi, Thatchenkery, Barrett, and Manning, 1994). This proposition simply means we cannot understand appropriate response patterns until we understand the lens of the actors.

Yet, shouldn't we *critically* examine the etiology and sustainability of those worldviews and resulting lens? No one wins when the outcries of people are ignored. If people have made the choice to wake up and rise up, I respectfully suggest that a new conversation should emerge. Equally important, I want to be clear that these examples are not relegated just to a country context. As we will visit throughout this book, organizations in varying forms are being either overtly or subtly impacted by people's fatigue with varying forms of marginalization. If you are the CEO of an organization that has a history of allowing people to feel disenfranchised, you will "feel" their wrath in their productivity, which impacts the organization's profitability! We no longer can look at the concepts of diversity, difference, and any other terms that we wish to associate with what differentiates people from a lens of dispassionate actions. More succinctly said,

> The peasant begins to get courage to overcome his dependence when he realizes that he is dependent. Until then, he goes along with the boss and says "What can I do? I'm only a peasant." (Friere, 2006, p. 61)

People are slowly but surely awakening to their dependence as they move toward independence and what it means to have their humanity valued. Yet, what appears to be taking leaders of organizations, countries, and other entities by surprise is this awakening, which is long past due.

When I think about diversity, intercultural differences, and how to effectively address many of these issues, I also cannot understand why we continue to address the issues of social injustice in developing countries from the lens of ethics and social responsibility. Is there that wide of a difference between the constructs that frame social responsibility versus valuing difference? We tend to neatly package issues into silo perspectives and propositions, thus failing to identify and address their relatedness, which can be germane to finding appropriate solutions. Yet, understanding the connectivity of issues is germane to evoking deep systemic change, or as adeptly stated by Dr. David Korten,

> Part of our inability to come to terms with institutional systems failure stems from the fact that television reduces political discourse to sound bites and academia organizations intellectual inquiry into narrowly specialized disciplines. Consequently, we become accustomed to dealing with complex issues in fragmented bits and pieces. Yet, we live in a complex world in which nearly every aspect of our lives is connected in some way with every other aspect. When we limit ourselves to fragmented approaches to dealing with systemic problems, it is not surprising that our solutions prove inadequate. If our species is to survive the predicaments we have created for ourselves, we must develop a capacity for whole systems thought and action. (Korten, 2001, p. 21)

If I have the ability to "see" humanity from the perspective of one-ness, would I, as a major corporate leader, even take my organi-zation down a path of importing human deprivation upon others simply because the people who are subjected are different from me, or worse, they are not in an economic position to protest? Does their difference imply my right to impose substandard working environ-ments and conditions upon them?

These are difficult questions that the literature typically wants to gingerly handle and/or address under separate domains. It is easy to find social justice addressed in its own respective literature or merged within the ethics literature. However, if we are to move past the silo mentalities that continue to frame our responses to complex ques-tions, we should learn to deconstruct and reconstruct issues from an interrelated systems perspective. In other words, the question needs to be continually asked that if people cannot "see" equality from their domestic lens, why should we expect them to act differently on a global level—a question that also challenges how we want to dif-ferentiate between diversity and intercultural management.

My perspective and point in writing this book is not to be politi-cally correct. Our world is in crisis. Even when we view events that are not in our backyards, we cannot walk away from the issues. The failure to value difference and people's humanity is a worldwide con-cern. In my own country, the United States, there is another level of civil war being raged.

Violence and the deaths of our most precious resources—our children are being addressed by lackluster attempts to ameliorate the conditions that are giving rise to their death tolls. In many ways these are issues that fall within the domains of diversity—or the lack thereof. You see, it was not until youth violence in the latter part of the twentieth century began to attack Caucasian communities that the discourse about "what to do" began to change. And, even with those tragedies, the death tolls of young people—particularly youth of color across the globe—continue to morph to unprec-edented levels. There is not one inhabited continent in our world that does not have youth gang problems, which suggests a serious breakdown of multiple systems that impact children. The level and intensity of interventions designed to ameliorate this issue will largely depend upon the demographics of the youth most impacted.

Yet a child, regardless of his or her ethnicity or race is too valuable to lose—children are our future!

The concepts and issues associated with valuing difference should be viewed beyond corporate domains. They reside on many levels and the resulting actions to "remediate" situations are inappropriately executed across many venues.

As I have taught diversity over the years, from the position of my lens as an active actor in this maze of diversity and as an individual who has nationally and internationally traveled and witnessed poverty, difference and many differentiating factors that give rise to class, socioeconomics and other domains of separation, I personally have grown in both my pragmatic perspectives and my understanding of human nature—an understanding that has reshaped how I view the topic of diversity and difference.

Over the course of these latter years, I have learned that no matter how sophisticated a change strategy one institutes in an organizational setting with respect to diversity and intercultural management, until we begin to have authentic conversations that address society's failure to embrace our humanity, regardless of our ethnicity, gender, or any other spectrum of difference, there would be little to no sustaining change.

Although I spent years in the corporate sector addressing diversity—experiences that are discussed within the context of this book that I pray helps frame productive cognitive dissonance in the reader, it was not until I began my walk through seminary and began to synthesize my seminarian training with my corporate background, business degrees, and experience in the "fields," that I "saw" diversity from a broader lens.

Historically, our world has continued to face a failure to evoke an egalitarian environment. You can easily trace the historical concepts of domination and power to contemporary times by utilizing examples such as the development of World Wars, the impact of toxic wastes upon developing countries, the expansion and growth of racism, of sexism, the exposure of children to violence, exacerbated by the proclivity of media and all other types of inputs to perpetrate the concept of redemptive violence as a guiding praxis for society (Wink, 1992). The issues do not simply reside within the walls of corporations—points I will address in later chapters.

Yet, power is not always bad. We need leaders, we need systems, and we need institutions. However, we need leaders, systems, and institutions that possess strong "interior spirits" (Wink, 1992). And, we will need those leaders who possess strong interior spirits to lead the charge as to how we value humanity across our various venues.

I believe that those that reside in the "C" suite will need to emerge as the *serious* leaders of change. In other words, it is time for them to change their standard operating procedures regarding diversity and intercultural management. It does not matter whether those leaders are CEOs of major corporations or the heads of NGOs or government entities. Their leadership and resources coupled with an enlightened insight regarding the need for change positions them to be the force that can begin a mass movement toward valuing humanity—a concept I address in my proposed model for change.

It is also important to understand that my point in writing this book is not to exhaust the literature, as I engage many issues that I "see" needing to be treated differently in the diversity conversations. I simply have the following propositions that are designed to evoke controversy in order to begin a very different dialogue:

- There are far too many issues of disenfranchisement that we continue to allow to exist globally throughout our world. They reside in multiple domains.
- Our responses and strategies to address these issues are insufficient.
- The way in which we understand issues of discrimination on multiple levels has to expand if our world is to productively survive and we are to reverse discrimination. Discrimination spans within the walls of corporate America, our educational systems, developing countries, and the list goes on!
- We must move beyond structural responses that tend to represent lackluster attempts to implement programmatic initiatives and move to strategies that embrace the humanity of all people—regardless of where they globally reside.
- And, we have to keep this forward movement going. We can no longer afford to be comfortable with our response patterns, because as I will point out in this book, close to 40 years after the enactment of varying civil rights laws just in the United

States, the issues remain unchanged and the same holds true for many other countries—a few of which are identified in varying chapters.

Unfortunately, organizations of many types globally struggle with accepting difference, and many even cite in the literature the proposition that diversity can have both positive *and* negative impacts (Seymen, 2006)—a proposition I have difficulty understanding.

For example, Dadfar and Gustavsson (1992, as cited in Seymen, 2006) suggested that there seemed to be a general agreement that if cultural diversity was managed well, it would be an asset to performance, and if overlooked or mismanaged it would diminish performance. Yet, Chevrier (2003, as cited in Seymen, 2006) suggested that diversity increased the ambiguity, complexity, and confusion in group processes and therefore could become potentially devastating for the effectiveness of teams in organizations (Seymen, 2006).

Interestingly, Harung and Harung (1995, as cited in Seymen, 2006) argued that the coexistence of two diametrically opposite qualities—diversity and unity—should be kept together for sake of a strong individual and a strong organization, further suggesting that the organization's diversity would lend itself toward a need to differentiate actions. Yet, this differentiation would ultimately lend itself to the organization's need to integrate these differences in support of achieving an organized effort (Seymen, 2006)—a proposition if developed within the "right" climate would privilege *both* the individual and the organization, however we want to identify the concept and construct of organization.

When the powers that lead our global society (be it government, corporations, or any other form of organizational structure) fail to create the climate that values humanity, or the differentiation noted by Harung and Harung, they are out of alignment. However, there is positive redemption through constructive transformation—a transformation that must move beyond band-aid approaches to profusely bleeding issues (Wink, 1992; Robinson-Easley, 2012).

Facing the Frustration of Change

I understand that my frustration with this topic and others that continue to stretch the social fabric of my country and other countries emanates from my bias as a trained professional in change management. Yet, I am also very grateful for the seminary training I have thus far experienced. My learning continues to reinforce the simple proposition that we cannot solve complex problems with simple solutions.

In this dynamic world we participate, there is no neutral ground. There is no choosing *not* to participate. Yet, individuation is important also. Awareness of one's "shadow" side is critical to effective participation, so is awareness of one's own "brokenness" (Wink, 1992). Leaders who may have failed to effectively value difference in the past are important to the change of the future. Privileging where one sits in the conversation of change from one's many lens and vantage points, particularly where one has learned from one's mistakes, is critical to effective participation and an ability to construct workable and result oriented change.

You see, I never shy away from my lens as a woman of color. I believe when we work to neutralize our understanding of the issues via the vantage point of being an active actor, we risk valuable perspectives—a point I address further on.

Six years following the completion of my doctoral dissertation, I began my walk through seminary, although it is not yet a completed journey. My experiences working in the "field" in concert with the seminarian training I have thus far received have helped me to understand that until I learned to touch and impact the hearts and souls of people who deal with oppression and hurt every day of their lives, whether it is oppression in the workplace, community, or any other venue, the most sophisticated change design in the world would not make a difference. The leaders of our many complex systems have to work to understand that the only way to positively progress in today's global society is to vision a change that embraces our humanity. With that said, I made the decision to write a book that approaches the topic of diversity from a different point of view.

We cannot continue to fool ourselves. Organizations, governments, and institutions of varying designs that fail to value diversity and intercultural differences are vastly becoming destructive entities. They are tearing down our economies, ecosystems, and prohibiting the flourishing of our developing neighbors.

Organizations that "play" with diversity and intercultural difference and pretend to invoke egalitarian environments are just as destructive. They play with people's feelings by invoking false expectations that the leadership will value them and their contributions irrespective of their "difference," thus setting forth the stage for alienation and the resulting backlash that has the potential to decimate an organization.

The Structure of This Book

As you read, you will see the evidence of my diversity journey from a very upfront and personal perspective. I intentionally insert myself into the conversation of how to evoke change in environments and ameliorate issues that are still dividing our global society. My first-person perspectives are very pronounced in this book and, as previously stated, I do not shy away from my lens as a woman of color. Yet, I am also a trained academic and scholar, which means I will also utilize a third-person perspective to provide an overview of the issues and current context.

In addition to my management training and experiences, as previously said, you as the reader will also "hear" my seminary training and experience. As I have said in my other books, book chapters, and journal articles—our hearts and souls have to heal, which is why I believe the literature on spirituality continues to grow. People across the world are searching for hopeful organizations and grounding in a context and environment where they see themselves valued and regarded as human beings without labels. Yet, far too often people express feeling summarily dismissed as inconsequential in the grander scheme of productivity and profitability.

There is also a suggested and detailed model for evoking change in our organizational environment. I hope, as the reader, you have grown as tired as I have of reading about issues of disparity, inequality, and all the other spectrums of "isms" that plague the globe, and are ready to step out on faith and evoke a different type of change strategy.

This model, however, might seem a bit prescriptive. In many respects it is because it represents my learning from my academic training and my work as a management professor in concert with a 20-plus-year career in the business sector where I have had the opportunity to witness and understand why change processes fail.

In the final chapters I also posit the application of this model, the theories, and praxes discussed throughout the book to a global audience and context. The issue of our failing to value people as human beings goes beyond the day-to-day interactions we face in the United States. As we examine and understand the many areas of disempowerment that agencies such as the United Nations continue to grapple with, you will see that those issues will not go away until we address our appreciation for people from a level that moves beyond relegating them to a profit margin equation.

Most important—mentally, spiritually, and physically walk with me as I urge our invoking a different series of paradigms that I believe from the deepest recesses of my heart, if assumed by people across the globe, will invoke a spiritual awakening to the beauty of mankind that far exceeds the need to invoke diversity, intercultural or any other type of "interventions," and change strategies designed to establish equality in multiple venues across our world. To evoke lasting change means that there will be times that we go against the wind. Or, as Oliver Wendell Holmes has put it, "To reach a port we must sail sometimes with the wind and sometimes against it. But we must not drift or lie at anchor."[2]

Acknowledgments

Once again, I give glory to my Creator for inspiring me to write this book. I give thanks once again to my friend and colleague, Mrs. Dortha Brown for her patience in reading as I wrote and challenging me when I needed that "kick." She continued to be a beacon of light when I needed to talk through the issues I was contemplating and researching.

I also give thanks to my children, Jodie and Caitlin, for their ongoing support. The way they live their lives and their resulting work gives me hope. I believe their generation will be the drivers of the change that will make a substantive difference in our world.

I also want to thank the editorial staff at Palgrave Macmillan; Charlotte Maiorana, Leila Campoli, and Sarah Lawrence. They saw and believed in the vision of this book.

I dedicate this book to the grand lady who mentored my writing but transitioned before its publication.

Introduction

My background as it pertains to diversity and other areas of management is quite diverse; an attribute I value since it has provided me with the opportunity to view the topic of diversity from multiple vantage points.

I have worked in the field of human resource management and organization development for close to 40 years—beginning with my undergraduate internships in labor relations, which occurred at the time when Title VII and other subsequent civil rights laws were signed into legislation. I held management and executive positions in human resource management where I had both human resource and organization development responsibilities in multiple sectors. During the last 19 years of my career, I have served in higher education. I am a tenured associate professor in management and have taught at the undergraduate, graduate, and doctoral levels. In addition, for over 20 years I have consulted to and trained a variety of organizations on the subject of diversity management.

Working, teaching, researching, publishing, and consulting in the areas of diversity have been of special interest to me. As a result, I have extensively explored the concept of difference from many perspectives. Yet, what continues plague me is how little progress we are making globally with respect to a topic that daily we live with.

Living with and understanding differences are core competencies that are germane to our growth as a global society. Yet, we still see inappropriate exchanges that emanate from people's inability to understand and value difference. The world of "difference" in today's global environment spans many dimensions and is not relegated just to race, sex, or ethnicity.

The purpose of this book is not to debate the topic of what constitutes difference or to privilege individual spectrums of difference. My goal in writing this book is to help people understand why the prevailing methodologies we continue to use over and over again when addressing difference no longer work for us in today's global environment. In other words, my goal is to deconstruct what we have done in the past and juxtapose this past to alternative lens and methodologies that privilege humanity.

One might question why I am so concerned with challenging methodologies and our prevailing lens. Over the course of my career in the professorate, I have had students at the graduate and undergraduate levels compare and contrast varying organizational environments with respect to their ability to effectively design and implement effective diversity management strategies. As a final team project at both the graduate and undergraduate level, I typically require that students assess how the organizational environments they review understand, design, and implement diversity strategies that help them successfully move their organizational strategy.

Yet, year after year far too many students have concluded that the organizations they chose to assess were not up to par in understanding what valuing difference really meant!

As I have taught intercultural management in the French West Indies at the graduate level for three years to business executives who live and work in the French West Indies, I am also amazed at how we have difficulty understanding the differences between diversity, intercultural management, and the resulting intercultural exchange processes.

For many people it is difficult to move seamlessly through the constructs associated with intercultural management because they simply cannot get past the blockages that impede their ability to effect an organizational environment that values diversity—ergo "difference" within their own individual contexts. Yet, we reside in a global village, which begs the question if people cannot acknowledge difference at home, how do we expect to effectively function in a global community that encompasses more cultural and microcultural differences than we can even begin to articulate?

Consequently, when I work through these topics, I may also address the dynamics of diversity and intercultural management at the same time. You see, I am not convinced—an argument that I hope to effectively make—that the differences we would like to associate with diversity versus intercultural-ism are in fact valid. I believe they are deeply intertwined and at best may simply reside on a continuum, which begins with one's ability to move beyond a mindset of compliance toward valuing difference within our own geographic context (diversity) to the ultimate acceptance level being working and operating in cultural environments that reside outside one's own geography and cultural context.

The Continuum of Compliance, Diversity and Intercultural Management—Are There Really Any Differences between These Concepts?

At the very lowest level of accepting difference are organizations that continue to have run-ins with regulatory agencies due to their inability to comply with the requirements of a nondiscriminatory work environment. As I have worked in and consulted to organizations in the United States, it does not surprise me that many cannot make the leap to valuing difference or effectively working in an intercultural environment. They are still stuck in a compliance mindset.

In addition to organizations being stuck in a compliance mindset is the dynamic of power, which can either reside as a separate organizational issue or complicate the compliance mindset even further.

Yes, there are people in organizations who have a problem with accepting anyone who looks different from them, yet I also have found, albeit anecdotally, that there are many issues associated with power and the dynamics of power that also contribute to the failure to import an egalitarian environment—hence my references early on in this book to the concept of power and domination.

You see, when an organization establishes a more equalized playing field, those individuals who have traditionally been in power lose some of that power and the resulting rewards associated with it. Consequently, when an organization makes available more influential positions to women or people of color, the individuals who have traditionally held those positions now have fewer positions to hold on to.

To emphasize this point, let us take a historical walk and look at the first case of reverse discrimination—Regents of the University of California *v.* Bakke, 438 U.S. 265 (1978).

This was a landmark 1970s Supreme Court case that was one of the first to bring to the public's attention the issues of "loss." Allan Bakke, a white graduate student, protested his inability to enter medical school at the University of California at Davis by arguing that affirmative action programs prevented him from entering and therefore were denying him his rights under the thirteenth and fourteenth amendments of the Constitution (http://score.rims.k12. ca.us/score_lessons/evolution_of_civilrights/bakke.htm, downloaded May 6, 2013).

The University of California Davis School of Medicine had set aside 16 of the 100 seats for "Blacks," "Chicanos," "Asians," and "American Indians," and established a separate admissions process for those 16 spaces. The "diversity in the classroom" justification for the policy of considering race as a factor in the admission process was different from the original purpose stated by University of California Davis School of Medicine, whose special admissions program under review was designed to ensure admissions of traditionally discriminated-against minorities (http://en.wikipedia.org/wiki/ Regents_of_the_University_of_California_v._Bakke, downloaded May 6, 2013).

The medical school originally developed the program to (1) reduce the historic deficit of traditionally disfavored minorities in medical schools and the medical profession, (2) counter the effects of societal discrimination, (3) increase the number of physicians who would practice in underserved communities, and (4) obtain the educational benefits that flowed from an ethnically diverse student body (http://en.wikipedia.org/wiki/Regents_of_the_University_of_ California_v._Bakke, downloaded May 6, 2013).

In a split 5–4 decision in favor of Bakke, the US Supreme Court said racial quotas must be eliminated. Supreme Court Justice Lewis Powell however stated that race can be a factor, but only one of many, to achieve a balance. In other words, race could not be a decisive factor in admitting or excluding applicants (http://en.wikipedia.org/ wiki/Regents_of_the_University_of_California_v._Bakke, downloaded May 6, 2013).

In the midst of asserting one's individual rights in this 1970s landscape, many overlooked the real reason behind this school's (and others that followed) reasons for invoking a set-aside plan—access for people who had traditionally been disenfranchised. Yet, in 2013 we continue to grapple with issues of disenfranchisement and equality of an educational school system where privileged communities versus inner-city communities (where people of color primarily reside) continue to expand the barriers of disenfranchisement. And, while "set-asides" is not a major focus today as it was during the Bakke case, the inequality of funding, school closings, and at the post-secondary levels, access and affordability for people who continue to face disempowerment are issues at the forefront for educators and policy makers who have the responsibility to address these issues.

The simple fact remains that despite all the presupposed progress we have made, there is still a need for "set-asides," albeit a new title may be associated with the concept.

Recently, participants on one of the list servers I belong to—that consist of academic colleagues of color in management—began an online discussion regarding a blog post in the New York Times that was written by another academic who has extensively studied inequality in the workplace. Her propositions, substantiated by her research are interesting:

> It's easy to believe the worst is over in the economic downturn. But for African-Americans, the pain continues — over 13 percent of Black workers are unemployed, nearly twice the national average. And that's not a new development: regardless of the economy, job prospects for African-Americans have long been significantly worse than for the country as a whole.
>
> The most obvious explanation for this entrenched disparity is racial discrimination. But in my research I have found a somewhat different culprit: favoritism. Getting an inside edge by using help from family and friends is a powerful, hidden force driving inequality in the United States.
>
> Such favoritism has a strong racial component. Through such seemingly innocuous networking, white Americans tend to help other whites, because social resources are concentrated among whites. If African-Americans are not part of the same networks, they will have a harder time finding decent jobs. (Ditomaso, 2013)

Can we truly "argue" with this statement? And, does the same hold true for others of color who have historically been in disadvantaged positions? Is the real question "Have we made significant progress?" Or is it "Are we continuing to have a conversation that speaks to individuals being traditionally excluded from the mainstream?"

Twenty-three years after the Bakke case, I wrote my first article on managing diversity, which will be addressed in later chapters. In that article I asked the reader to imagine Company XYZ, an organization that had been historically a Caucasian male dominated organization and had done little in the way of recruiting into the organization people who were different (including women). Yet, recent economic and business issues caused this organization to rethink the demographic makeup of its workforce (Easley, 2001). The organization had to expand into new markets, which included Hispanic and African American markets and was also considering global expansion. Therefore, to accomplish new organizational strategic initiatives, the leadership decided to actively and aggressively recruit women and people of color (Easley, 2001). To insure that this demographic shift in the organization was successfully accomplished, the leadership planned to engage in diversity training while also developing managerial development programs for the women and people of color who were assessed as having high potential (Easley, 2001).

Sounds familiar? Perhaps one could respectfully suggest, 23 years later, that this was just another variation on the same theme of The University of California Davis School of Medicine reason for invoking their special admissions playbook?

Yet, in this case and countless others that followed, the organization cited as an example did not examine its underlying assumptions regarding diversity in the workforce. The organization did not deconstruct the learned behavior of the Caucasian males as they progressed through the organization, nor did they closely examine the leadership's behaviors that validated this lack of diversity (Easley, 2001).

Consequently, one could assume that since the behavioral practice of noninclusion prevailed in this organization, that the group norms, espoused values, formal philosophy, rules of the game, climate, embedded skills, habits of thinking, and shared meanings were never challenged with respect to how they reinforced the paradigm that diversity was not previously needed—until it became a business necessity within this organization (Schein, 1992, as cited in Easley, 2001). Yet, despite it becoming a business necessity, when a senior-level executive challenged the sexual harassment of a female member of his team with a client, he was the one facing discipline because the client was too valuable to lose.

Unfortunately, when I revisited this organization a few years after I wrote this article, the force of economic change proved not to be a sufficient motivator for changing the organization's culture from one of no inclusion to a very different paradigm where was valued because of the deeply embedded culture (Easley, 2001). This example and countless others we could cite only proved that the strategies that often are designed to enable an organization to manage diversity tend to become weak attempts to put band-aid approaches on profusely bleeding issues.

Eight years later, Groschl examined a group of major international hotel organizations and analyzed their corporate diversity management statements and policies. He found that the majority of language used to describe their diversity management strategies and initiatives was not grounded in making a business case, but was grounded in a language of antidiscrimination related claims (Groschl, 2011). Yet, as we continue to move through the twenty-first century, we cannot forget that globalization has played a key role in the widespread movement of migrant workers across the globe.

Australia is just one example of a country that has 25 percent of its national population listed as foreign-born (Bissett, 2004). These numbers make it hard for people to differentiate between diversity and intercultural management strategies. Are the core competencies of organizational leaders and their respective management teams different for invoking an equalitarian environment, managing diversity, and/or developing an organizational culture and context that can effectively function in an intercultural environment? I think not!

A significant task of management is to understand and consider the social-cultural situations and developments, such as customs, habits, and codes of conduct, and their influence on human behavior (Neuert, Opel, and Schaupp, 2002), which means everyone is not going to be the "same"—diversity or difference will bear multiple iterations.

Consequently, organizations seeking to evoke change should seek to understand how their workforce is grounded in both epistemology and ontological reasoning—which goes back to my 2001 assumptions that you have to understand the culture and all of its antecedents (Robinson-Easley, 2013)!

When investigating workforce diversity issues in Turkey, Ozgener found the dimensions of discrimination to be vast. Demographic characteristics, sociocultural structures, managerial policies and behaviors, union tendencies, regional differences, laws, and local community, in concert with gender, educational, age differences, and political opinions all influenced discriminatory practices in medium-sized businesses in Turkey—a country where diversity investigations are not as extensive as they are in other countries (Ozgener, 2008). Yet, if we were to deconstruct these antecedents, we might find their possessing deeply grounded epistemological and ontological roots.

Understanding the epistemology and ontological reasoning are critical competencies for diversity managers charged with the responsibility to design and evoke the change. Actions and strategies of diversity managers are framed and/or limited by situational and relational factors that reside within and those that are external to the organization (Tatli and Ozbligin, 2009). Situational factors address the web of organizational and social structures and power relations that mold that organization in its social and organizational fields (Tatli and Ozbligin, 2009). Therefore, this web of organizational and social structures and power relations, influenced by both internal and external variables, can impact how change is evoked in the organization, which means merely engaging in diversity training and/or the more structurally oriented processes of expanding recruitment efforts can be exercises in futility.

The mere existence of these complex antecedents and relationships can render diversity managers as *constrained* agents of change (Tatli and Ozbligin, 2009). Diversity managers have to navigate through the varying webs of relationships that exist at micro, meso, and macro levels, which require understanding individuals and organizations as *relational* beings that are intertwined in a constant process of emergence and becoming (Tatli and Ozbligin, 2009).

Moving Past the Issues of Constraint

I believe that if we are ever to move past the blockages we continue to manifest regarding our ability to seamlessly work in, benefit from, and equally important enjoy the kaleidoscopic hues and many realms of people, we have to move past constructing answers that are grounded in *structurally* designed strategies and examine transcending past our biases in order to understand difference from a perspective that binds humanity.

As a first step in understanding the complexity of journeying to this ultimate acceptance of difference, I will set context by walking you, the reader, through my experiences with the topic from my varying lens.

You see, I did not emerge with a different understanding of difference by virtue of suddenly waking up and "seeing" the light, or even through my personal experiences as a woman of color. Similar to the organizational examples I cite, I had to learn through many trials and errors. Yet, I was open to learning and made a conscious choice to challenge prevailing paradigms that did not appear to work. I learned to privilege my multiple lens—that of a woman of color, a trained change strategist, a seminarian, and any other descriptors that ontologically inform how I view my world.

My varying roles in corporate America and now in academia have provided many opportunities to examine the concept of difference and varying intervention strategies from the inside out. And, my walk through seminary has had a profound impact on my understanding issues of marginalization from a very different vantage point as well. Throughout the years, I have designed diversity strategies, wrote journal articles and book chapters on my learning, and engaged in countless training strategies. Yet, as I look back on each of those experiences, they all fell short of the real goal of valuing humanity.

When I wrote those articles, I was just as guilty of designing the same *structurally* focused intervention strategies that I now criticize. Consequently, I am not the least bit reticent in saying that these approaches do not yield the deep systemic change we badly need in today's global world.

We should learn to honor the humanity of people regardless of difference. Recently, at a presentation at my university, the Rev. Dr. Michael L. Pfleger said "We never integrated dignity and respect. In God's eyes, every life is a valuable life."[1]

It is no longer sufficient to say that organizations' primary focus on diversity should be to use the arrays of difference to maximize profitability, which is the typical justification for imposing expensive diversity strategies. And, we can no longer utilize the mantra of optimizing the organization when we close our eyes to the atrocities that prevail in developing countries that go beyond dehumanizing workers by requiring them to work in conditions that defy logic. These atrocities are linked to our inability to value difference. They require the same sensitivities and love for humanity—but they are rarely addressed in the diversity literature!

If organizations are to succeed in today's twenty-first-century environment, we need to allow the human spirit to flourish without binding it. Variations on this theme have been bantered around for a while. In 1992, social researchers Leinberger and Tucker suggested that the possibility and hope for community within organizations would lie in the everyday working assumption that one is far more profoundly and mysteriously connected to other people (Nichols, 1994).

If we agree with this proposition, is it safe to assume that the concept of human connectivity may clearly transcend beyond tolerating equality and insuring equal employment opportunity compliance? If so, why do far too many organizations still battle these "issues"?

The EEOC in the United States is not out of business nor are the varying state regulatory agencies. In fact, their case loads still flourish. Are organizational leaders who believe in the need to "manage diversity" working from a limiting paradigm regarding the value of people? How many organizations globally can honestly say they have moved beyond the need to "manage" difference and understand the value proposition of connecting to the soul of the worker?

The Expanding Landscape of Difference

Harung and Harung's 1995 proposition that the coexistence of diversity and unity should be kept together, for a strong individual and a strong organization merits much consideration (Seymen, 2006), yet requires a very different mindset that will need to transition beyond the limitations we now endure. Unfortunately, when reviewing the diversity literature, even in today's twenty-first century, there are indications that organizations across multiple venues and equally disturbing, varying countries, continue to grapple with the expanding concept of difference.

For example, in 2007, researchers examining the hospitality industry noted how, in regions such as the Republic of Ireland, Northern Ireland, and Scotland, the hospitality industry experienced a surge in workers coming in from various countries. The authors saw a need to address this diversity by better preparing students who are being trained to work in this industry. More specifically, it was suggested that institutions of higher education where these students train should infuse into their curriculum information that addresses the continuums of diversity and culture (Hearns, Devine, and Baum, 2007).

The authors also suggested that multiculturism may need to be understood not only as a training for competencies geared toward managing diversity, but rather as a process of educating students and staff for integration into an intercultural working environment. They saw colleges and universities that offer hospitality and tourism programs as vehicles that can readily support learning in these areas by providing greater focus within their curricular on legal and other aspects of multiculturalism and multiethnicity (Hearns et al., 2007).

While I believe that there is value to their propositions, interestingly, the institutions that Hearns et al. charged with the responsibility to build diversity and intercultural management curriculum—colleges and universities—continue to undergo scrutiny with respect to how they invoke diversity strategies into their own organizational environments. For example, when investigating the literature on how colleges and universities advanced campus diversity, it was found that prevalent strategies included diversity councils, vision and mission statements, strategic plans, committees and task forces, allocation of resources, and evaluations—each considered to be structural endeavors (Kezar, Eckel, Contreras-McGavin, and Quaye, 2007).

Equally concerning in Hearns et al.'s recommendations was the need to concurrently focus on the legal aspects of multiculturalism and multiethnicity (2007). Unfortunately, organizations' propensity to primarily focus on the legal aspects of difference is still at the forefront of many leaders' minds.

When you simply focus on understanding and/or implementing the laws, you miss the opportunity to drive systemic change. Therefore, implementing programmatic initiatives that address legal compliance can only hinder an organization and/or country in its attempts to stay current with a continually morphing world.

To this point, in Australia the focus of EEO legislation was predominately upon women. And, while organizational policies have primarily focused on increasing employment opportunities for women, with considerably less emphasis on ethnic minorities and other groups identified as disadvantaged, the emphasis on women still failed to make significant strides (Syed and Kramar, 2010). Over a 20-year period, from 1985 to 2005, women's participation in the Australian workforce increased by 11 percent. However, while women in Australia comprise approximately 44 percent of the workforce, they hold a very small percentage of senior decision making roles in organizations (Syed and Kramar, 2010), suggesting the possibility that antidiscrimination laws have had a limited effect in facilitating cultural and attitudinal change in organizations (Pyke, 2005, as cited in Syed and Kramar, 2010). The gamut of strategies across public and private sector organizations in Australia appear to run from attempts to conciliate complaints behind closed doors to structuring the business case—particularly in Australia's corporate sector (Thornton, 2006; Bertone and Leahy, 2001; Coleman 1995, as cited in Syed and Kramar, 2010). Yet, when structuring the business case, are you helping those that still work on the fringes feel valued?

When surveying 1500 organizations in Australia, it was found that more than 51 percent did not have a written policy on diversity in concert with a lack of integration of diversity management into human resource management strategies. Many CEOs were also found to rank diversity policies and training significantly lower in importance than EEO (Syed and Kramar, 2010).

Maxwell discussed similar issues in Scotland's efforts toward managing diversity, noting that the lack of equality for individuals from marginalized groups can be seen in labor market figures (Maxwell, 2004). Yet, in 2002, it was reported that Scotland had 42,000 economically active people from ethnic minorities, mainly Asians living in Scotland, with approximately 13,000 living in Glasgow (Nomis, 2002, as cited in Maxwell, 2004). However, despite the high profile diversity public awareness campaign launched in 2002 in Scotland, during that same time period the Trade Union Congress reported that the Black and Asian unemployment rate was 12 percent compared to 5 percent for whites in the United Kingdom (2004).

Similarly, Black and Asian employees were reported to be largely excluded from senior management and Asian women faced a double problem of ethnicity and gender discrimination (Maxwell, 2004). Interestingly, the impetus for organizations to even address diversity can often be complex. Dobbin, Kim, and Kalev examined the organizational determinants of diversity programs and suggested that industry norms, corporate culture, and identity group power were the leading predictors as to whether or not organizations (after the 1980s) would even adopt diversity strategies (2011).

The global extensiveness of these issues is evident when examining the British National Health Service, which is the one of the largest employers in Europe. Approximately 38 percent of the total medical and dental staff in the British National Health Service is from Black and minority ethnic backgrounds, with 32 percent being overseas qualified (Healy and Oikelome, 2007). Yet, despite the percentage of Black and minority ethnic physicians and dentists, the researchers found that many of the physicians and dentists still faced growing evidence of discrimination to the point that it was possible that their careers and livelihoods were being jeopardized simply because they had the wrong name and wrong color of skin (Healy and Oikelome, 2007). However, the recommended response to importing equality into the system was to build national identity networks, which largely resembled diversity councils in the United States that also represented structural answers to a looming issue of an environment's inability to value difference.

In the twenty-first-century global economy, with extended and mobile markets and labor systems, the premises underlying affirmative action and equal employment law in concert with the original concepts associated with diversity management may need to be revisited in order to move beyond how these concepts are being co-opted (Watson, Spoonley, and Fitzgerald, 2009). Furthermore, when we speak on the concept of diversity, we should acknowledge the fact that the concept has morphed to include both local and international workforces, a diverse national and international multicultural customer base (that can easily be accessed via technology), and diverse international competitors (Watson, Spoonley, and Fitzgerald, 2009). For example, when examining the workforce in New Zealand, one in five New Zealand residents are overseas-born, putting the country ahead of Canada and just behind Australia (2009).

Perhaps businesses and employer/employee work organizations should manage and work collaboratively within the multilayered nature of contemporary diversity to solve complex problems and to create a competitive edge in the lucrative international marketplace where diversity itself is an accepted dimension (Watson, Spoonley, and Fitzgerald, 2009). Unfortunately, these are not new propositions and as a result beg the question as to why in today's global environment they are still being posited as innovative opportunities.

Dr. Peter Drucker, considered to be one of the leading contributors to modern management, extensively explored major demographic themes and their potential impact upon what was considered to be in the 1980s a more homogenous American workforce (Oyler and Pryor, 2009).

Drucker argued,

> Economists, businessmen and politicians have always known that population matters. But they usually paid no further attention—and were usually justified in doing so. For population shifts tended to occur on a time scale that made them irrelevant to the decisions businessmen or politicians have to make ... But during the second half of the twentieth century, the time span of population changes mutated. Population changes now are occurring within exceedingly short time periods. And population changes have become radical, erratic, contradictory—yet more predictable than anything else. (Drucker, 1980, p. 77, as cited in Oyler and Pryor, 2009, p. 434)

Consequently, managers and organizations were advised by Drucker to prepare for these trends, become vigilant and adaptive for sudden change, and develop strategies to take advantage of these new realities in order to make opportunities out of turbulent times (Oyler and Pryor, 2009).

As I have studied and taught management and leadership over the years, I have not lost hope because I know there are those organizations and their respective leaders that understand the foundational constructs of what Drucker proposed and what is written in this book. For example, Anita Roddick, founder and group managing director of The Body Shop embodied a transcendence philosophy that centers around the need to create a sense of holism and spiritual development in concert with insuring that their people are connected to the workplace, environment, and in relationship with one another (Nichols, 1994). I know we can find many cases of others on the global frontier. Unfortunately, the problems seem to be overshadowed by the far too many organizations that are not doing enough.

Expanding the Concept of Difference and Its Role in Contemporary Organizations

In a later chapter, I will address the ethical dilemmas that people are exposed to within the United States and globally, which tends to be relegated simply to the topic of social responsibility and/or bad ethics. The travesties—gross travesties—that people all over the world experience at the hands of organizational leaders are directly tied to a lack of respect for humanity. In other words, there are too many organizations that have globally expanded that fail to value difference and place people regardless of their ethnicity, gender, or culture on the same value scale as they would place themselves. If we learn to look at people as "less than," it becomes far easier to impose impossible work conditions upon women, children, and other members of the global community under the umbrella of doing business! After all, what they now have in wages is more than what they had in the past. Yet, does that give people the right to impose less than humane conditions upon the workers?

Understanding the Concept of "the Lens of Color"

As previously alluded to, over the years, as a woman of color who became very comfortable with privileging my color and lens, I have also learned to view the issues I will address from the vantage point of a very active actor in the landscape of diversity.

Frankly, I do not shy away from inserting myself into this conversation. Yet, as evidenced by my review of the literature, I am just as comfortable as a scholar in examining the conversation within this book from a scholarly perspective. Both positions are critical in an effort to heighten our sensemaking.

Knowledge and how we act upon our knowledge is linguistically and relationally constructed, which infers that it is almost impossible to ignore the role of the researcher. Not only do researchers play a role in constructing what they discover as reality; their theoretical sensitivities affect how data are collected as well as analyzed (Barrett, Thomas, and Hocevar, 1995). First-person perspective can be very valuable when examining one's own theoretical sensitivity in order to understand how the researcher's and/or consultant's identity, culture, and diversity attributes affect perception of the situation, the design of an intervention strategy, or evoke an understanding of how their interpretive schemas impact results (Easley, 2010).

Often when conducting and analyzing inquiry, our attempts to be value neutral are actually conducted within a field of values (Allen and Hardin, 2001). However, I believe an ability to effectively understand the feelings of people who perceive themselves to be marginalized, regardless of the level of marginalization, requires reaching deep into theoretical sensitivity.

Therefore, when we openly acknowledge our personal qualities and experiences, we also open space for another level of a consciousness of meaning to enter that can be subtle yet of significant impact when deconstructing how we create and manage sense and meaning (Pettigrew, 1979). I also believe that when we openly acknowledge our personal qualities, we can also open space for moving to a level of consciousness that incorporates our moral consciousness in concert with our pragmatic views. A higher level of consciousness helps us move beyond our individuality toward an awareness of our interconnectedness and mutuality with all of humanity (Marques, 2008). A higher level of consciousness also leads us to what Fr. Pfleger noted in his 2013 address at my university as a "divine tension."[2]

Evidence suggests that there are some organizations that understand the need to work toward operationalizing these perspectives. For example,

> Articulated through a post-Fordist discourse, organizations attempt to construct a "new times" workplace with the expectation that self-actualized workers will provide the company with the requisite market edge. A form of mutualism is sought, where both employers and employees share an ethic of care and sense of responsibility in relation to their working relationships: reintroducing a pre-modern "moral" basis to the employment contract. A raft of management literature refers to companies attempting to build such a sense of community, frequently framed as a "postmodern spiritual future for work." Recognition of difference, and a celebration of diversity in general, is said to be integral to this awakening of the importance of human identity and its relationship to identification. The implication is that the post-industrial context is one where culture supersedes the machine as a central motif, guiding both working relationships and the global experience of market exchange. (Bissett, 2004, pp. 315–316)

If we are to move past structurally applied intervention strategies with respect to understanding, valuing, and managing difference, and move toward the "postmodern spiritual future for work," we have to learn to privilege our individual perspectives, which can be very enlightening for us, simply because honoring the self is the forerunner to honoring the collective—honoring humanity.

I have often questioned students as to why they believe that diversity initiatives fail. We are often quick to point the finger at the easy answers, but sometimes it is the subtleness of power and the varying behavioral dynamics of people who currently hold the organization's power that can definitely impact the success of diversity and intercultural management activities in organizational environments. Another dynamic to consider, as my students in Guadeloupe have so eloquently and collectively summarized in their many treatises on the subject; those that are charged with managing difference often fail to understand the varying layers and historical contexts that inform the actors within the organization and their respective interlocutors.

Understanding the more subtle nuances of difference is critical when looking to move beyond prevailing paradigms. Comprehensively understanding our world is said to emanate from our activity, which produces a social context that defines who we are (Davies, 1991). Yet when researching, and/or constructing change initiatives, we often do not acknowledge our multiple roles that definitively impact our views—that of subjectively coherent participants in jointly produced story lines and that of an objective participant (1991).

When we focus on moving to a higher level of consciousness, we also start to broaden our perspectives and examine the well-being of life in general in everything we do, while concomitantly rethinking our job, its contents, the organization where we work, its mission, and most importantly our behavior toward our colleagues, friends, and loved ones (Marques, 2008). The potential outcomes—we become aware that meaning is crucial in making our life's journey a pleasant one for others and ourselves and just as importantly, we start engaging in ways to create meaning (2008).

In doing so, we reach out to others no matter how they differ, we deviate from positional protectionism, political friction, and selfishness in our daily actions working to evolve toward the things that are really important—a purpose in everything we do and a sustainability for all life on earth (2008)! Therefore, working toward the collective organizational good via integration as suggested by Harung and Harung (Seymen, 2006) is indeed possible through the valuing of one's diversity. These concepts do not have to be mutually exclusive. Yet, they clearly require a different mindset and organizational structure in order to effectively work. Therefore to fully argue my case for alternative perspectives and paradigms regarding difference in our work and social contexts, I have to be both the objective participant who has no problem in deconstructing both mine and other's lackluster attempts toward "managing diversity" in order to disclose the etiologies of those lackluster attempts, as well as that of a subjective participant whose paradigmatic perspectives can help frame the constructs for the mutual inclusion of diversity and unity.

Each perspective has its own individual vantage point. You see, it is within those lines of subjectivity as an actor who has designed and implemented lackluster attempts to manage diversity that I can "see" and feel—in the deepest recesses of my soul—why our prevailing paradigms regarding difference and resulting strategies do not work. Yet, it is also enlightening being a part of the organizational population for whom diversity strategies are aimed. It is hard for me to truly understand marginalization unless at some level I have "felt" that emotion.

When we dig deep into ourselves, we will find that each of us would have felt marginalized at some point in our lives—even those who appear to compromise the "majority" population. However, when we examine successful leaders, we often find that the individuals who run the more successful organizations that value humanity are people who openly acknowledge and talk about conditions they never want their workers to experience because they "know" what it feels like.

The questions I ask throughout this book result from many years of being in the position to be an actor in the various "scenes of diversity" from a variety of positions. The socially constructed venues in which I have worked and/or lived in clearly give rise to my guiding praxes. As a PhD in organization development who possesses a scholar–practitioner focus due to many years in the corporate business sector, I am trained to systemically assess and deconstruct situations and identify, develop, and design systemic change strategies that move those situations (e.g., organizations and systems) toward a desired state. However, I am also layered with many other microcultures that inform my views.

Therefore, when privileging my lens as I deconstruct those layers, it is appropriate for me to first acknowledge that I am an African American woman who comes from a collective African consciousness (Easley, 2010). As a result, my theoretical sensitivities emerge from a place where issues of duality and objectification in the background have been historical themes in my life, which have also impacted my personal and professional life (Easley, 2010). Consequently, strategies that in reality are not designed to invoke an egalitarian environment are easily disclosed when you are the actor supposing to be on the receiving end of change.

My experiences with the lack of diversity strategies in a workplace and their impact upon my professional career spans not only my corporate life, but life in the academy as well. These perspectives inform my views toward transcending beyond the barriers I have personally experienced.

While the majority of my expertise in the area of diversity management will emanate from my 20-plus years' career as a practitioner in business, in my academic career I have also had the opportunity to experience diversity issues from a different vantage point, which was discussed in my 2011 contributing article to the book, *The Black Professorate: Negotiating a Habitable Space*. As I began to write my chapter for this book, I struggled with whether or not I should be politically correct. Yet,

> When the opportunity came to write on the topic *The Black Professorate: Negotiating a Habitable Space*, as I began to write, I focused on maintaining objectivity and not allowing my real feelings to influence what I felt needed to be said. Initially I privileged being politically correct versus my simply stating the issues in concert with proposed change strategies. However, as I read what I wrote, it clearly did not reflect how I authentically address issues in my research and publications. After all, did I dare risk offending my colleagues? But most important, what I initially wrote did not address the multitude of emotions I feel about being a woman of color in higher education. Higher education was a place where I initially thought that if you had a mission to serve and educate students, work to be recognized in your respective discipline, serve your institution, community and surrounding stakeholders, while working hard to accomplish the

criteria for performance, tenure and promotion, you would be successful in achieving your goals. I never imagined as I made the decision to switch careers that higher education has just as many barriers as the business sector I left. (Easley, 2011, p. 45)

What was more troubling to me was to "hear" the voices of my colleagues who also contributed to this book. Their experiences were eye opening. And, the review of the literature in preparation for this book chapter was just as troubling. Despite having received one of the highest degrees offered in our country, transitioning to positions where we were theoretically held as subject experts, you still heard the pain of marginalization from individuals of color in the academy.

I am also a former seminarian who was trained in seminary to more critically examine the epistemology, ontology, hermeneutics, and root metaphors of a change strategy juxtaposed against the environments in which we work (Easley, 2010). As a result of the many layers of my microcultures, I have become increasingly more uncomfortable with the application of traditional change theories and praxes. I now understand that the theoretical sensitivities and lens through which we tend to view individuals and organizational constructs may be unconsciously as well as consciously limited even when we attempt to take a *neutral* position (Easley, 2010).

When I made my decision to apply to seminary in 2004, my focus was on social justice. I felt very positive with the decision to choose Chicago Theological Seminary (fondly known as CTS) because of their historical social justice stance. It was an added plus for me that CTS was affiliated with my religious denomination. Yet, what I did not know was that CTS was one of the first seminaries to be open and accepting to the LGBT community. Therefore, when I began my walk through seminary, I found myself to have another layer of minority status imposed upon me—that of a heterosexual female in a community of seminarians where the predominate population was not heterosexual students.

The years I spent with my colleagues increased my sensitivities toward difference. I heard their pain at levels I never before understood. The bashing and marginalizing they experienced in multiple contexts caused many to initially question their relationship with their Creator. In other words, questions such as "Does God love me because I am different" would routinely emerge. And, as I got to know the LGBT community of color in my seminary, my sensitivities toward understanding the additional layers of difference grew once more. While it can be very challenging, as an African American woman of color, to acknowledge the many aspects of duality I daily face, if I were a lesbian woman of color I would be in an even more complex space with respect to the barriers I have to navigate.

I also learned that when we chose to address difference and the valuing of humanity, we have to incorporate inclusion at all levels. As I was wrapping up a book chapter I had written for the book *Women of Color: Taking Their Rightful Place in Leadership*, (the chapter was titled "Easing Our Path: The Healing Power of Dialogue for African American Women in Leadership") one of the editors asked why I didn't include the lens of lesbian women in my chapter. Despite my "sensitivities" toward difference, my first "gut" response was, "I am not a lesbian woman of color, so how can I adequately represent their voice in my chapter?"

The truth was, I had not even thought of including their voice until I was questioned. As a result, I researched as well as incorporated what I had thus far been learning as I matriculated through seminary and the pictures were not "pretty." The point—even those who face being excluded can and do exclude others, thus exponentially expanding the concept of "othering." As a result, it was important for me to learn that,

> Change without unity can be challenging. Yet historically African American women who have chosen to live their lives as lesbians and bisexual individuals have faced a triple threat of oppression: being forced to work through issues of race, gender, and sexual orientation. And, while it has been posited that living the life of a lesbian is a life that draws its strength, support and direction from women (Reynolds and Powell, 1981), recent studies suggest that marginalization within the African American community is sometimes higher than that within the white communities, with Black women who regularly attend church displaying higher instances of homophobia than their male counterparts. (Negy and Eisenman, 2005; Redmond, 2006), (Robinson-Easley, 2010, pp. 224–225)

Should we always have to be "called out" or should we understand the need to incorporate the voice and perspectives of people from all walks of life? For me, being questioned regarding my failure to be inclusive was a valuable lesson—one that I hope to never have to relearn. My years at seminary taught me at a different level to remove labels and look into my seminarian colleagues' hearts and souls as a community of oneness. Simply, we were a community of people committed to the ministry of social justice. And, it was our oneness with respect to our humanity that gave us the opportunity to make a difference in our world.

Movement beyond barriers should be our global society's primary goal—a movement that entails our embracing a higher level of consciousness toward humanity; a commitment to openly move beyond barriers that will eventually nullify the need for conversations on "managing" diversity, understanding intercultural differences, and, equally important, a movement that positions us beyond the need to work through issues of child labor, sweatshops, and all other forms of industrial practices that appear to negate the humanity of people across the globe.

Learning to value people on the basis of their humanity is not a new concept. Yet, to critically understand it, one should understand the personal lens of those who feel dominated and subjected to all the "isms" that run parallel to our definitions of difference. I respectfully suggest that learning to value humanity requires organizations to move to a different level of spirituality.

Spirituality in the Workplace

When we simply look at the topic of spirituality in the workplace and its connection to valuing humanity, we see a literature that continues to grow. Moving beyond the academic literature and expanding into the trade literature as well, people are suggesting that the concept of spirituality and optimal human development have direct impact upon organizational performance, productivity, and profitability.

What really is this connection to spiritually and its relationship in embracing humanity? Why is this connection a better perspective than "managing diversity"? Why should organizational leaders even care enough to go to this level of paradigmatic change toward their workforce? After all, in today's economic environment where jobs are steadily being cut, is not it enough that an individual has a job?

Spirituality and its connection to humanity includes the basic feeling of being connected with one's self, others, the transcendental—the universe. It is a feeling that *energizes* action. This connection moves an organization toward ultimate values, which, if achieved, will make the global ethical travesties previously mentioned unthinkable. And, this connection fosters the recognition of an inner life that nourishes and is nourished by meaningful work in the context of community. Lastly, this connection helps to move people toward personal envisioned growth (Mohamed, Wisnieski, Askar, and Syed, 2004).

When workers are encouraged in their workplace to self-actualize; thereby realizing one's highest "self," (e.g. linking issues of transcendence toward ultimate values via privileging one's personal context, history, cultural values, and lens—ergo their microcultures) they become far more valuable to their organization. The organization does not have to work through the many disconnects between an organization and their workforce because of broken trust, psychological contracts, and feelings of being undervalued. For example, in the United States, for far too long the perceived breaking of psychological contracts, exacerbated by increased layoffs have continued to negatively impact organizational productivity and profitability. Many people feel devalued in their organizations—a feeling that can and will manifest itself into the workforce's output, thereby directly impacting productivity and profitability.

Years ago, my human resource colleagues and I were working with a diversity consultant at a time when diversity training was just becoming "popular." Upon completing her employee interviews and debriefing us, she asked if we had a problem with our product becoming rusted. We responded "Yes," and that the manufacturing department could not figure out why. She responded that the employees were so angry with the organization that they were urinating on the product to "get back at us." I never forgot that incident and others that I encountered in my years consulting where organizations would face significant backlash when people felt devalued.

At some point, we have to continue reiterating a need for a "healing" between workers and their respective employers—which I believe begins with the organization recognizing the individualities of their respective workforce. This healing is particularly important due to the demographic shift in the makeup of today's workforce.

Similar to Dr. Drucker's propositions on the demographic change that was coming, just seven years after his treatise on the topic, Johnston and Packer (1987), who worked with the Hudson Institute, a major think tank organization, suggested changing demographics of the US workforce that would statistically equalize the playing field for women. Yet, over a quarter of a century later, women still make (in the same jobs) less than men. Their projections also identified the rapid growth of Hispanics in our workforce and other ethnic immigrants—projected outcomes that I began to see actualize while recruiting in the 1990s.

Globalization is expanding recruiting boundaries without requiring individuals to relocate. And, the literature on how to manage intercultural relationships continues to grow. Therefore, as we invoke diversity strategies from multiple contexts, be it the lens of diversity, multiculturalism, or any other socially appropriate term we wish to apply, we should simultaneously question our ability to understand the respective actors from their many layered social and cultural perspectives—their lens.

Our willingness to engage in also understanding their hearts and souls will help answer the question as to whether we should intentionally use more culturally appropriate points of reference for developing strategies of change that help people feel liberated in multiple environmental contexts while also empowering them to reach their fullest potential (Hopkins, 2005). Our ability to provide a transcendent view of difference is the only way I believe we will *effectively* grow as a global society. Equally important, as we work to provide a transcendent view of difference, it should be an authentic effort and not one ensconced in programmatic initiatives. Our failure to engage in an authentic transcendent view of difference can only result in a shallow understanding of people and equally shallow change oriented strategies; or as the Rev. Dr. Martin Luther King Jr. noted, "Shallow understanding from people of good will is more frustrating than absolute misunderstanding from people of ill will. Lukewarm acceptance is much more bewildering than outright rejection."[3]

As we explore concepts and constructs that may personally challenge you as the reader, I also respectfully ask that you, like me, insert yourself into the dialogue in this book, from the subjective perspective as the reader. Embrace, challenge, and/or argue with what I say.

Similar to what I always tell my students, it is through an engaged discourse that we learn. Even if you do not agree with everything that is written in this book, make the commitment to understand that there are many different ways of examining and understanding the multiple aspects of the issues. Perhaps in the simple act of reading something that challenges your guiding praxis, you will entertain options other than those that have typically resided in your comfort zones.

To state my case, I am going to take the liberty of first walking the reader through my experiences in the design and management of diversity strategies over the course of my career.

My intent in doing so is not to "tout" my writing. While I believe I had many critical insights that were published and interestingly to me are still cited in the literature, I have taken those insights and deconstructed them in order to emerge with new paradigms that are more relevant to today's global context.

Therefore, part 1 of this book will walk the reader through my historical experiences with diversity and the resulting change strategies and models that I individually and in collaboration designed. Do not get me wrong. I believe that there are still critical concepts embedded in my work that hold value in today's context. However, they should be expanded to fit the dynamics in which we now live, points that I will address in part 2.

I learned a few years ago from two researchers and scholars in the field of organization development—people whose research and publications are internationally well known and who are revered as prominent scholars—that the true measure of a scholar is his or her ability to question their praxes in light of a dynamic and changing environment. While there are many constructs that are foundational to our reality and will remain tried and true, there are equally as many that need to be critically examined—and changed!

So, walk with me as I tear apart my past perspectives and ride with me on the wave of change. Our world is so exciting, which means we cannot afford to wallow in stagnation. Very simply, "Change your thoughts and you change your world,"—Norman Vincent Peale.[4]

Part I

My Journey and Understanding of Diversity and Intercultural Management from the Lens of Traditional Paradigms

CHAPTER ONE

UNDERSTANDING DIVERSITY FROM THE MINDSET OF A STRUCTURAL APPROACH TO CHANGE

Educated and trained in human resource management and organization development, I historically approached diversity from a pragmatic mind set. Yet, over the years I have learned that if individuals, organizations, countries, and global economies are to "make" diversity work in people's daily lives, they have to embrace a mindset that transcends the traditional concepts of difference and resulting implementation strategies.

Throughout my travels, I have been exposed to a number of different cultures and contexts. As a result, my views on the concept of difference have been dramatically challenged. For example, I learned when working with international colleagues that the ordering of country culture, ethnicity, and ultimately race significantly varies and, as a result, impacts the individual's perceived identity in ways you typically do not find expressed in the United States. Consequently, the concept of diversity is viewed from a very different context.

I embrace this change and continue to challenge my students to embrace different paradigmatic views on the concept of and constructs associated with difference especially when they examine the application of organizational change in concert with understanding how diversity can and does impact their self-efficacy, growth, and development.

The Mindset of Affirmative Action and Compliance with Equal Employment Opportunity Laws

I have also learned that the lowest level of work I had to do with regard to the concept of difference was dealing with affirmative action issues and their resulting legal ramifications. And, even in the twenty-first century, I still have to deal with issues of compliance and teach these constructs in the classroom.

While I am very well trained in the legal landscape of affirmative action and equal employment opportunity, each time I have had to "defend" a case for my organization in a regulatory hearing, or teach a class and hear students speak of their personal struggles with issues of inequality, I have struggled with understanding why organizations cannot evoke an egalitarian environment—despite their affirming to be an equal opportunity employer. What is it about difference that compels people to act in such a negative manner? Yet, over the years, I have also learned that the issues associated with equal employment opportunity are far more salient than just an organization's inability to embrace difference.

In 2001, as I attempted to work through the cognitive dissonance I felt, I wrote:

> To meet the demands of today's technologically advanced society, organizations must rethink what diversity means and how the concepts of developing, valuing and managing a truly diverse organization must transcend traditional strategies. The traditional practices of engaging in programmatic initiatives to address diversity, such as diversity training, recruiting and hiring people from different backgrounds may not be appropriate for this millennium. New strategies, which incorporate successful, sustainable, and systemic organizational change processes are required to keep up with the systemic change that is impacting our world. These new strategies will need to incorporate organizational transformation, where in the deepest recesses of an organization, diversity becomes an internalized and realized part of the organization's culture, norms and value systems and is displayed in every aspect of how an organization interacts and manages the workforce. (Easley, 2001, pp. 38–39)

Yet today, 12 years later, organizations still struggle with basic issues of compliance, which begs the question as to why, in this millennium, we still keep regulatory agencies in business. More succinctly said:

> Twenty years later as we progress through a new millennium the reasons for addressing diversity are also changing. The advent of the twenty-first century, incorporated with technological advancements have broken many barriers which impact the way and frequency of

how people in this world interact and communicate. The brick and mortar walls, which served as traditional barriers to working with people from different cultural backgrounds, are quickly being eliminated. As a result, in today's technologically advanced environment, it is not unreasonable to think of an organization hiring a department from another country without those workers ever having to leave their location, or a college professor teaching students from all over the world in one internet classroom environment. Technology makes these types of human interactive arrangements possible. (Easley, 2001, p. 38)

If the walls and resulting barriers that separate people have been broken, why can't we break down the mental walls that still invoke unwarranted issues with regard to our worldwide and very diverse workforces?

Diversity Management: Still a Valid Concept?

Despite this being a cliché, as we continue to move through the twenty-first century, the one constancy we continue to face is the rapidity of change. Traditional boundaries that were our previous comfort zones, separating people across many barriers such as country, region, or workforce, no longer exist. Our boundaries are global and our workforce is global, and as a result, there is a broader continuum regarding difference that organizations must navigate. While diversity management has traditionally been addressed from a localized context, intercultural management has traditionally assumed the international business focus. The literature continues to subtext these issues and their relative competencies and skills from different contexts.

The international business arena now forces intercultural competence at the individual level and is presumed to be associated with global career success. At the organizational level, intercultural competence is associated with business success (Morley and Cerdin, 2010). Yet, in the face of this change, we still approach understanding diversity and difference from traditional paradigms, which do not ready us for a rapidly changing landscape of difference.

Twelve years ago, I pondered if organizational leaders in the United States had actually learned how to build a true diverse culture that values difference, or if we, as a global society, are in a

..c sophisticated stage of compliance. Twelve years later, I am not comfortable with asserting that we have made the level of strides necessary to position us as global leaders in the landscape of understanding and navigating through difference.

In 1997, it was suggested that traditional barriers to diversity, which were easier to identify 20 years ago, had been replaced by more subtle forms that are embodied in traditional values, which provide us with comfort (Brief, Buttram, Reizensten, Pugh, Callahan, McCline, and Vaslow, 1997). In 2013, that is still a valid proposition. Yet, globalization and technology continues to connect people together in ways that were previously thought impossible; connections that result in new definitions and dimensions associated with the term "diversity" (Alvarez-Pompilius and Easley, 2003).

These connections have caused me to continue to ponder over whether egalitarianism, diversity, equity, justice, and intercultural competency are terms that represent varying dimensions of the same construct and are positioned along a singular continuum relative to requisite competencies. Can a true egalitarian context in which culturally competent people work exist when issues still emerge regarding basic respect for and management of difference, whether it is diversity of the people, diversity of organizational cultures, or a combination of both? (Easley and Alvarez-Pompilius, 2003).

In the earlier stages of my career, I felt comfortable separating the concepts of diversity, diversity management, affirmative action and intercultural competence. However, there are definite vantage points to age and experience; I no longer separate these concepts.

My experiences have taught me that the ability to effectively manage diversity on the home front requires the same skill set, heart, ethics, and respect as when managing in an intercultural environment.

So, how did I come to this conclusion? My personal epiphany did not occur overnight. While I had authored and/or coauthored other works on diversity, I believed my first "serious" work on the topic was the article previously addressed, "Developing, Valuing and Managing Diversity in the New Millennium," which appeared in 2001 in the *Organization Development Journal* (see figure 1.1). Having a combined practitioner and scholar focus, I began to research and challenge prevailing assumptions and dialogues with respect to what constituted the effective management of diversity.

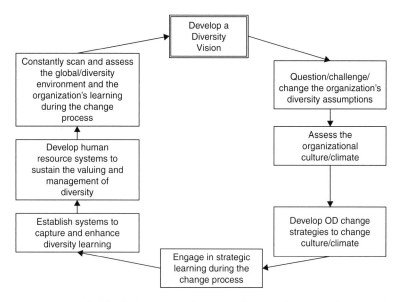

Figure 1.1 Model, Easley, 2001—Roadmap for Developing, Valuing, and Managing Diversity in the New Millennium.

Source: Easley, C.A., (2001). "Developing, Valuing and Managing Diversity in the New Millennium," *The Organization Development Journal* 19(4) (Winter 2001).

When I began working through the diversity questions that continued to plague me, I drew heavily upon my experiences in the corporate business sector. I have learned over the years that "he (and for sake of inclusion, I add)/ she who dares to teach must never cease to learn" (Richard Henry Dana Jr.).[1]

Over the years, I had witnessed organizations spending considerable sums of money on sensitivity training and diversity management programs. Yet, even when they were successful in recruiting a diverse population of individuals into the organizations, they struggled with retaining the people they recruited. Strategies such as diversity councils, focus groups, and similar types of endeavors to "hear" the voices of the underserved and underpopulated organizational members only served to anger people more. It was simply window dressing. Workers from diverse backgrounds would take considerable risk in joining these councils because they believed in the individuals who were championing their cause.

I soon began to understand that because many of the champions did not work in levels of the organizational structure that would allow them to be the drivers of real change, these initiatives had little impact upon the organization. The champions echoed in good consciousness and beliefs the concerns of their peers, but the real change would reside at the leadership levels of the organization—in the "C" suite and these were typically not the individuals attending these meetings with their workforce.

Even when I factored in that both sensitivity training and diversity management initiatives were fairly new strategies in organizations at that time, there still appeared to be something missing when these strategies were used. One of the more glaring questions those of us in human resources would ask was—how long would results be sustained?

When I wrote the *Organization Development Journal* article, I incorporated a model that was designed to move an organization toward effectively valuing and managing diversity. The conceptual framework of the model challenged traditional intervention strategies, such as training and suggested a multidimensional approach to changing an organization's culture. The model also included assessment and intervention strategies aligned with processes designed to institutionalize the change; processes that were built upon organizational learning theory (Easley, 2001).

My criticism of training as a preferred diversity strategy was straightforward and was based upon my practical experience in the workplace and educational grounding in training and development. I also incorporated the perspectives of other researchers who also closely studied the effectiveness of diversity training. The critique of training as a preferred diversity strategy grew and, as a result, in the mid-1990s the literature that resulted from practitioners and scholars critiquing diversity training programs began to look robust.

During this time, the thinness of the empirical research was criticized by many researchers. Many questioned the real effectiveness of traditional interventions, the lack of clear objectives for the training initiatives, and the ongoing failures to give managers tangible standards for understanding how to interact with people from different cultural backgrounds. There were researchers who also suggested that the training programs yielded little change in day-to-day behaviors. Inclusively, many thought that the training strategies used resulted in increased hostile behaviors such as backlash, reinforcement of group stereotypes, post-training discomfort and group infighting (Golembiewski,1995; Grossman, 2000; Rynes, and Rosen, 1995; Paskoff, 1996).

I suggested in my 2001 journal article that change strategies as they related to diversity could not just be addressed in the context of training and recruitment initiatives. To properly understand the appropriateness of diversity interventions, one would need to delve deeper into the organizational issues. I also noted a need for organization leaders to discuss and come to grips with the organization's commitments to the human element as part of their strategic decision making processes, inviting organizational members to the table when designing change processes.

During the same time frame, I worked on a consulting engagement where I was asked to provide diversity training to over 1,000 employees within a state organization. This organization had serious legal issues and was under a consent decree, which meant that their prior diversity initiatives had obvious flaws—points that will be further expanded in a later chapter.

Working with this organization brought to light other perspectives. As I suggested earlier, the subtle issues that drive people to suppress others will often emanate from spaces and perceptions of systems of domination—racism, class elitism, sexism, and imperialism—systems that should be acknowledged as behaviors capable of wounding the spirit (hooks, 1995).

Unfortunately, damaged spirits rarely choose liberation and/or change (hooks, 1995). We cannot ignore these realities because they drive the need for us to intentionally utilize our cultural points of reference for developing an attitude of liberation, whether it is from a personal and/or an organizational context (Hopkins, 2005). We should also factor in that when the organization wounds the spirit of the workforce, whether intentionally or not, they risk a psychological disconnect that will ultimately impact the organization's effectiveness, which also impacts the organization's ability to economically thrive. You see, organizational leaders should understand how their workers see themselves being oppressed.

Some say there is a duality in oppressed people. On one level they are themselves, and on another level they represent the image of the oppressor that they have internalized (Friere, 2006). I saw this duality in my working with this state agency and within other organizations I later worked with.

What has continued to intrigue me as I walked through seminary and examined various literatures, is that power and domination are common themes across far too many organizational and cultural contexts (Robinson-Easley, 2012). It is also quite interesting to examine how these varying cultures grapple with their status in life. For example, from my own lens, African Americans have been told that they are less than their white counterparts. Even in the midst of the abolishment of laws that eliminated the inability of African Americans to equally participate in the various institutions of life, we still get messages that we are not equals in this society (Robinson-Easley, 2012). Yet, it is not until those who see themselves being oppressed concretely discover their oppressor and in turn their own consciousness that they move past a fatalistic attitude toward their situation (Friere, 2006).

Therefore, when organizations are serious about evoking an environment that values difference, they have to be ready to move their membership to a space that allows them to be all that they are meant to be. This movement should be endorsed and led by the leadership of the organization. Yet, training initiatives rarely took organizations to this level, and they clearly were not designed to address the subtle and/or overt power dynamics that were contributing to the perceptions of oppression. As a matter of fact, I saw far too many cases where the sensitivity training backfired, largely due to a failure to manage the reconciliation processes that were needed to heal the open wounds that emerged during this training.

To better understand the dimensions and dynamics of our respective situations and the associated psychologies of privilege, our approach to change should push the limitations of a traditional conversation and propositions in order to develop strategies that privilege our ethno-narrative understanding in our approach. In this open space we need to also feel the freedom to deconstruct our implicit feelings embedded in our settings, context, and social interactions (Foucault, 1986; Hansen, 2006; Easley, 2011). While sensitivity training opened space for those feeling marginalized, in sessions I attended I saw the individuals who were characterized as part of the oppressing "group" shut down; thus a one-sided dialogue typically ensued.

While in 2001 I intuitively understood these concepts, I had not completely deconstructed them from a theoretical perspective. Yet, at this stage of my "diversity" career, I began growing more uncomfortable with current approaches to managing diversity. I believed and wrote that if organizations were going to fully internalize diversity, should perhaps a precursor to their diversity vision be their questioning through deconstructive dialogues their assumptions about the people, their culture, and the value of those differences? (Easley, 2001; Golembiewski, 1989). However, the modality for structuring these dialogues would have to be structurally different from the traditional sensitivity and diversity training formats.

I was also beginning to understand that resistant behaviors toward change and control can be interpreted as "symbolic violence" (Oakes, Townley, and Cooper, 1998), which occurs because the actor's stability in a professional specific cultural context is threatened—again the emergence of issues of power, domination and/or loss of power and control, juxtaposed with the duality of rage. Symbolic violence coupled with the shutdowns that could occur during sensitivity training sessions could only lead to more negative and divisive behaviors. Yet, despite these many propositions there was still a flaw in my thinking—which now I understand. While there is significant value to the model from the context of driving change at the organizational level, real progress with EEO, diversity, and intercultural management begins within the hearts and souls of the individuals who are *responsible* for the organization as well as with those who work in the organization. In many respects, those who work in organizations where they have faced significant marginalization remind me of the people and resulting behaviors so adeptly described by the late Paulo Freire. You see, what I believe is most important regarding Freire's work is that he saw *liberation* in the hearts and souls of those marginalized. It was simply a matter of time before they incurred an awakening.

> Liberation is thus a child birth, and a painful one. The man or woman who emerges is a new person, viable only as the oppressor-oppressed contradiction is superseded by the humanization of all people. Or to put it another way, the solution of this contradiction is born in the labor which brings into the world this new being: no longer oppressor no longer oppressed, but human in the process of achieving freedom. (Freire, 2006, p. 61)

Deconstructing the Concept of Difference

Through collaborative research and other publication initiatives following my 2001 article, my learning once again morphed to another level. Following my diversity work using Appreciative Inquiry, which is described in a later chapter, a colleague and I began collaborating on the topics of diversity, organizational culture, identity and change and the varying versions and intersections of these concepts.

Alvarez, in her groundbreaking work with culture and change in France found behaviors in the organizations she studied, which reinforced Oakes et al.'s propositions on organizational resistance. Her work explored diversity from the vantage point of microcultural issues and their respective impact upon organizational change efforts.

In France, Dr. Alvarez examined one of the largest reorganizations ever conducted in the public healthcare system in France at that time (Alvarez, 2001). The merger associated with the Georges Pompidou European Hospital (HEGP) gathered people from three hospitals, each possessing their own "organizational" culture. One of the objectives of the merger was to provide a proximity hospital for the current needs of nearer populations while concurrently developing a highly specialized hospital with medical poles of excellence (Alvarez, 2001 and 2002; Alvarez-Pompilius and Easley, 2003).

The merger focused on building a "patient-centered organization" to favor a patient global quality care process. The innovative changing forms of the hospital's organization and structuring reshaped the relationships between controllers and clinicians, thus modifying power equilibrium, impacting microcultures and therefore the organizational culture (Alvarez-Pompilius and Easley, 2003; Alvarez, 2001).

The study explored the consequences of the merger on individuals' and groups' representations regarding change, control, and information exchange, and also analyzed cultural perspectives relative to the underlying premises of trust and its impact upon the receptiveness to management controls and change (Alvarez, 2001). To evaluate the representations of organizational control, the cultural impact of the merger, and the success of the change process, Alvarez focused on individuals, groups, and organizational levels, utilizing content analysis of data, which resulted from detailed qualitative interviewing. Attention was paid to the "situated meaning" of the elements of discourse obtained through interviews (2001).

Data that examined why the behaviors of the organization were counterproductive to the successful implementation of management control strategies suggested that the first level of understanding relative to the hospitals' workforce included how those actors interpreted the structural aspects of the merger within the context of country culture, and the resulting political systems and hierarchy (Alvarez-Pompilius and Easley, 2003; Alvarez, 2001 and 2002).

Alvarez found that the different professional groups (headquarters, local administration, doctors, nurses) developed particular sets of practices and specific representations of change and control and that there also existed professional cultures, which possessed expressions of diversity inside each of these cultural groups—findings that raised significant questions for Dr. Alvarez and me with respect to whether or not we truly understood the many dimensions of diversity (Alvarez-Pompilius and Easley, 2003; Alvarez, 2001and 2002).

Her data suggested additional impacting layers of diversity that included proclivities associated with professional behaviors and practices, augmented by gender, and other variations of difference, all of which impacted the interpretive schema of the actors and resulted in the formation of the culture of the resulting merged hospital (Alvarez-Pompilius and Easley, 2003; Alvarez, 2001 and 2002). The failure of the organizational leadership's ability to understand these issues resulted in a merger that took close to 20 years. One had to ask, albeit in retrospect, if these varying microcultures had really been understood, would there have been the same levels of difficulties and resulting time delays?

What is interesting to me, as I have worked for several years within the French culture, is that there is an overriding concept of being "French" first, which in the minds of many people I have encountered appears to override the nuances of differences. Yet, France extends beyond the borders of the country and entails departments, such as the various islands in the French Caribbean, which makes diversity in France quite interesting.

Dr. Alvarez's data strongly suggested the need to move beyond a singularly focused view of organizational culture and diversity. However, to effectively compare and contrast the meaning of this data and its importance when developing diversity strategies, let us first examine the model I proposed in my 2001 *Organization Development Journal* article, which did not incorporate the level of analysis posited by Dr. Alvarez. This model had a multidimensional approach that included the following steps:

a. Develop a diversity vision as a part of the organization's mission and strategy that identifies the benefits of a diversity workforce and where the organization sees its future state relative to diversity.

b. Assess the organization's existing culture (and subcultures) through in-depth culture/climate assessments. Utilize multiple assessment tools and triangulate the results of those tools to validate the data. Based upon the outcomes of that data continue to delve even deeper into the organization in order to understand, from a phenomenological perspective, the values, beliefs, shared assumptions, and psychological contracts of the organization and how they impact behavior and diversity initiatives.

c. Question the organization's assumptions about people from varying cultures and ethnicities.

d. Be prepared to challenge and change those assumptions. Within the context of questioning, include assessment tools that will evaluate the organization's diversity assumptions. Triangulate this data with the data that emerges from the organizational culture assessments.

e. Develop the organization development strategies that will work to change the culture and the resulting behaviors that impede change in general in addition to a successful diversity strategy. The outcomes of the culture audits will suggest the appropriate OD strategies and starting points within the organization. Where possible and appropriate, utilize OD strategies that include collaboration, which facilitates organizational ownership.

f. During and after the OD change processes, engage in strategic learning, which also begins to establish a learning environment that values risk taking and open inquiry and dialogue with respect to diversity.

g. Within the context of learning about difference, establish systems to capture and disseminate the learning throughout the organization through other organizational processes. (Easley, 2001)

The model heavily focused on the concept of organizational culture, yet from a very traditional lens and suggested that when we look to transform an organization's perspective on diversity, we also have to explore the organization's shared basic assumptions and how they impact the socialization processes within an organization and also explore how these assumptions are taught to new members (Easley, 2001).

Within the context of this model was the proposition that understanding the shared basic assumptions would also shed light on the organization's operating paradigms, psychological contracts, and value systems of the leadership, all of which, if uncovered, would provide change strategists with a deeper understanding of what a diversity strategy should entail (Easley, 2001). Yet, Alvarez's work proved otherwise.

Deeply understanding the organization's culture was believed to be foundational to understanding what were priority issues for leaders within the organization due to the interaction between leadership and culture; leaders create and change cultures. Yet, I later realized that at that stage of my professional development, I still viewed organizational culture from a lens that was too narrow. I really did not understand until a year later that I needed to better question what really constituted the concept of organizational culture. I needed to further explore whether culture and diversity exist, from a phenomenological perspective, on two sides of perhaps the same coin (Alvarez-Pompilius and Easley, 2003).

When the concept of culture was initially conceptualized as a critical part of this diversity change model, a theoretical premise of the model suggested that to empower a diverse workforce to reach their full potential, the organizational *system* needs to be changed and the *core culture* modified (Thomas, 1991; Easley, 2001). The model also suggested that inherent in the concept of modifying the core culture was the need to develop an understanding of the values that operate within the organization from the leadership throughout the organization to the societal myths that the organization has internalized. Culture, in this sense was simply defined as a pattern of shared basic assumptions that the organization has learned as it solved its problems of external adaptation and internal integration (Schein, 1992).

CHAPTER TWO
THE BEGINNING: MOVING DIVERSITY STRATEGIES BEYOND STRUCTURAL INTERVENTIONS

> *When the remembered promises press for the liberation of people and for the humanizing of their relationships, the reverse of this thesis is true: everything depends upon interpreting these transformations critically. The way of political hermeneutics cannot go one-sidedly from reflection to action. That would be pure idealism. The resulting action would become blind. Instead, this hermeneutic must bind reflection and action together thus requiring reflection in the action as well as action in the reflection. The hermeneutical method to which this leads is called in the "ecumenical discussion" the action-reflection method.*
>
> —Moltmann, 2006, p. 44

Understanding the relationship between action and reflection as referenced by Dr. Moltmann is critical to intellectual growth. I often tell the story to my students of how Dr. Alvarez and I met and the perceptions that would emerge when she and I would walk into an organization and/or academic environment. We first met in England at an organizational discourse conference. What drew us to begin talking to one another as quickly as we did was our being the only people of color in the room. Although Dr. Alvarez is a French citizen, born, raised, and educated in France, her family originated from Haiti. Consequently, our skin colors are of similar hues—which typically is one's first identifier of difference. One of our common denominators, or microcultures, was that both of us are trained in the fields of organizational behavior and organization development. Yet, color and educational orientation were largely our only points of commonality when we first met. Noticing, acknowledging, and learning from the reactions of people when we would be together formed, as Moltmann describes, our action-reflective learning processes, which were germane to our research on diversity. What we soon learned was that despite those similarities, our differences were many. She had both European and Caribbean life experiences, and had taught in more international contexts than me—microcultures that informed her perspectives. We had language differences and she was married, as was I, but I was also a mother with two children. I was 18 years her senior, was born and raised in the United States, and possessed over 20 years of work experience compared to her beginning to teach soon after she finished her doctoral program—once again, microcultural differences that informed how we engaged our work.

Yet, because we both were deeply committed to our work, we learned to use our differences as leverages to better understand the environments in which we worked and taught; but most importantly, we used those differences to explore the multiple contexts associated with the construct of "difference."

As we collaborated with our work, we also raised the question as to whether or not we (and others) had oversimplified the concept of organizational culture as it pertained to diversity. Since much of my work was in challenged communities across the country, I asked the same question for that context as well—a point that will be later explained. In the writing that followed our research we began to suggest that if we were to understand organizational change from a diversity lens, a global framework should integrate the issues of diversity and culture in a *dynamic* relationship (Alvarez-Pompilius and Easley, 2003), which was a different treatment of culture from my 2001 model.

As a result, we began to explore what a model would look like that expressed the social dynamics between microcultures and diversity attributes as parts of the overall organizational culture. At the 2003 IFSAM/SAM World Congress, we left fellow academics with the question: What forms the basis for shared values and to what extent are those values really shared or does the organization move through reflexive/reflective processes of integration (through microcultures) and differentiation (through diversity claims) that ultimately results in some type of grouping which we then call the culture? (Alvarez-Pompilius and Easley, 2003).

We questioned how many layers of difference actually make up individuals and how stable is the resulting culture, as we have traditionally defined it. Do the dynamics of socialization, enrichment, and learning, which are built upon the concept of differences, tend to make culture malleable to change more than we have previously thought?

Theorists have tended to suggest that while changing the culture is possible, it clearly is not one of the easiest organizational tasks, which begs the question: Is changing the culture difficult because we don't truly understand its linkages to diversity? (Alvarez-Pompilius and Easley, 2003).

We suggested that when looking for answers for how to move an organization toward valuing diversity, it becomes critical to utilize organizational assessment strategies that examine deep structures within the organization, which are primarily the interpretive schemas in actor's minds.

To examine these deep structures calls for examining, at a deep and discursive level, the individuals who make up the organization, which enables a better understanding of central themes, root or generative metaphors, as well as rhetorical strategies, all of which contribute to the various levels of culture as posited (Bastein, McPhee, and Bolton, 1995; Kets de Vries, and Miller, 1987; Thatchenkery, 1992; Alvarez-Pompilius and Easley, 2003).

As a result, our modeling of these concepts morphed once again. When we began to explore these issues with colleagues at the World Congress, we emerged with a model that expressed our concept and constructs relative to microcultures.

We also realized that my original 2001 model, where I had simplified researching the organizational culture, now had to be supplanted with the inclusion of this component, which made researching and understanding the organizational culture a far more complex—yet necessary—endeavor. While there are theoretical underpinnings and methodologies in organization development that open space for the reflection-reflexive modeling noted in the beginning of this chapter by Moltmann, a leading thinker in systematic theology, I believe that when we engage in reflection and reflective action, we should also include a conversation that addresses a detailed examination of issues, the environments, *and* internalized beliefs in order to better understand the psychodynamics of our praxes (Robinson-Easley, 2012). In other words, we have to better understand the propositions of Friere (2006) if we are going to move people who already perceive that they are working in disempowered environments to a space where they are able to internalize and embrace the organization; from a place of truly wanting to see it succeed versus simply "working" at a job.

We therefore suggested that keeping a coherent and global focus required integrated methodological processes to analytically identify patterns of microcultures and diversity and to manage them toward an emerging organizational culture as defined in the organization's change project (Alvarez-Pompilius, and Easley, 2003). A couple of years later, I found that the same concept was true when working within African American communities. Even though I bore the same ethnic and racial profiles as the people I worked with, their many microcultures, which resulted from significant regional differences, greatly impacted my ability to effectively work within their cultural context, despite our racial commonalities. Consequently, I quickly learned that before I even conceptualize approaching any type of organizational context, I should engage in extensive research in order to understand varying microcultures and their impact upon the larger cultural context—a topic I will visit in a later chapter.

As I have continued to work with colleagues, I am more convinced of the merit of our research on microcultures and the resulting propositions. The work I have done in the French West Indies led colleagues and me to begin a book project that is designed to bring forth a deeper understanding of diversity and intercultural management within the French West Indies. Dr. Alvarez and I are coediting this book, and the primary contributors are practitioners—mid to upper level managers in government, NGOs, and corporate environments who daily have to work through the many layers of difference and identity ensconced within the French culture and understand how these layers impact organizational effectiveness in the French Caribbean. Whether the actors in this cultural context are born in the French West Indies or have migrated from France, there is uniformity in agreement that the cultural context that, willingly or not, informs the relationship between workers and their leadership is a context that should be deeply understood and deconstructed. What intrigues me is that this is a continuation of the academic conversation that Dr. Alvarez and I began in the early 2000s. Yet, here she and I both stand, over a decade later, once again writing about it as if we had just begun the dialogue.

You see, while many may identify themselves as "French" first, there are far too many microcultural differences that reside within the inhabitants of the French West Indies to simply relegate interactions to one common denominator. There are layers associated with identity formation that result from their historical context of being initially a colonized people, which is also impacted by their African slavery heritage, in concert with a Creole background—overarched by their being "French." Yet, when white workers come from France and take jobs as managers and/or leaders in organizations, subtle conflicts have and continue to emerge because of a lack of understanding of these respective identity formations.

My students, who daily grapple with these issues from a human resource management perspective, know and have stated that the issues are not simply addressed by invoking structural diversity interventions. In each of their contributions to the book we are writing, they call for a deep discursive understanding of what constitutes those many layers and a need for organizational leaders and their respective workforce to engage in productive conversations around the concept and constructs of sensemaking with respect to understanding and factoring in difference, even though they each suggest a different modality for evoking that type of dialogue/intervention. At the bottom line, it does not matter how the conversations ensue; their point is that the conversations need to occur in order to move Guadeloupe to a different economic status in the French Caribbean.

While their propositions are indigenous to the issues we are addressing for Guadeloupe, I respectfully submit to you they bear significance to organizational environments worldwide. Yet, what continues to concern me is that the questions and learning discussed in mine and Dr. Alvarez's work and by my students in Guadeloupe, which are not salient issues, are still being addressed in the literature as emerging thoughts, which leads to the inference that we may still have a long way to go toward our understanding of how to value difference.

Chapter Three
My Early Work: Appreciative Inquiry as a Diversity Intervention Strategy

A little over three years ago, I was contacted by another academic from England regarding my work with Appreciative Inquiry as a diversity intervention strategy. This person also happened to be a journal editor and asked if I was interested in publishing the paper, which had been presented at a conference a few years prior. He viewed the paper as being ready for the peer-review publication process. I declined the offer, although I very much appreciated his offer. I did not feel that the paper accurately reflected where I now am in my understanding of what really constitutes a sound diversity intervention strategy. I have always been leery of academics who intentionally publish in stages, or are oblivious to where they are in their personal development for the sake of publishing, and as a result have worked to not fall into either trap.

Yes, learning does begin in stages, and yes, as I am sharing with you my learning over the past years regarding difference, which also has grown in stages. If I am to be true to self and my responsibility as a researcher, I have to deconstruct and incorporate into my praxes the additional variables I now see in the maze of diversity in order to understand how those variables can and do impact proposed change strategies.

However, the most important learning for me, and I hope for others as they read, is that it is okay to say that what you originally posited may need to be modified in order to stay current with the changes that are manifesting in our lives. It is when you chose not to challenge yourself that you do injustice to your work.

I had the unfortunate experience a few years ago of witnessing how some colleagues extend the dissemination of critical information for what appears to be very selfish reasons. It was an international venue. I was in a session that was being presented by one of my US colleagues who was describing a change process she and others had developed. The institution that this person was affiliated with had strong governmental ties. When we possess a doctoral degree, our responsibility is to bring new knowledge to our field, but I am learning that perhaps the additional terminology that should be used is inclusive knowledge (Robinson-Easley, 2012).

As I listened to her, to the trained ear it was quite apparent that critical components were missing in their model. So, I raised my hand and asked if they had considered these components, to which they said "Yes ... but that was next year's research." I never forgot that session (Robinson-Easley, 2012, p. 138).

When organizations, communities and any other entity that is working toward change relies on our production of knowledge to help them conceptualize and contextualize what needs to occur, we do not have the luxury of waiting a year to give them the complete picture, especially if we know in advance what that complete picture looks like (Robinson-Easley, 2012). Inclusively, if we have an idea that our prior theories have indeed changed to the point of requiring alteration, we need to convey that information as well. Self-serving needs relative to publication are inappropriate. We also do not have the luxury of time to "play" with the current flavor of the month. Far too many organizations have gone through that process, which yields little to no result (Robinson-Easley, 2012).

Appreciative Inquiry as a Driver for Diversity Strategies

The paper for which the invitation was extended described one of my diversity training programs using Appreciative Inquiry as an intervention, which was presented at the 2002 Midwest Academy of Management Conference.

As I continued my journey that began with my 2001 publication, the gnawing feeling that something might be missing continued. I continued to see organizations "announce" that diversity was going to be a primary initiative within their organization, and as a result they would engage in training or increase their hiring of a more diverse workforce. While those were typical responses, they continued to demonstrate a lack of *sustaining* change. Problems with retention would often emerge because the new employees quickly became disillusioned when they understood the real organizational strategies with diversity.

When I was doing this work, it seemed as though I was still searching for a way to connect the human spirit to an organizational change initiative. I kept revisiting the question/proposition that if organizations were to survive a rapidly changing diverse and global workforce and economy and sustain advantage, thus outpacing their competition, what strategies would have to emerge that would allow leaders to truly transcend their organization beyond the boundaries of traditional diversity initiatives? Similar to others' perspectives that were beginning to be strongly reflected within the literature, I did not believe that the traditional strategies that were at that time (and still are) being used were comprehensive enough to drive the real change that organizations require and these strategies would only result in standardized and/or quick fix approaches, thus helping organizations remain traditional in their diversity outlook (Loden, 1996).

The survival of organizations in our rapidly expanding global market continues to depend on how effectively they are managing and valuing difference, which translates into *understanding* the complex organizational issues that block successful diversity management. Those that investigate diversity strategies continue to support the proposition that the complexity of our workforce and continual expansion of organizations into global markets are bringing forth far greater diversity challenges, which may be why titles such as "Chief Diversity Officer" still exist in today's global environment.

I do not believe anyone can argue with the value proposition that effectively valuing and managing diversity will enhance an organization's performance by positioning the organization to (1) attract and retain the best available human talent, (2) enhance problem solving, (3) enhance marketing efforts, (4) facilitate higher creativity and innovation, and (5) provide more organizational flexibility (Cox and Blake, 1991; Cox, 1994; Brief, Buttram, Reizensten, Pugh, Callahan, McCline, and Vaslow, 1997). Yet, is there more to effectively valuing and managing diversity? When we truly embrace difference, what can viscerally happen within an organization that will suspend the managing element of diversity and move it to a level where the organization flourishes as a result of the composition of its varying hues? Isn't it true that when you plant beds of flowers, the more beautiful beds are the ones that are a mixture of types?

Yet, in today's current environment, as in the 1980s and 1990s, research results on diversity training programs challenged the rationale for focusing on the individual in the organization versus addressing organizational systems (Hayles and Russell, 1997). When we view the organizational system, we cannot step away from understanding the *human dynamics* that make up that system. Yet, getting to the core of those human dynamics can be challenging. Despite those challenges, it is still prudent to ask whether it is now time for organizations to move beyond structural change strategies and understand the nuances and layers of the human spirit in order to properly align the mind, body, and spirit of a workforce with the ultimate intent of truly connecting people to the organization's core strategies and programmatic initiatives.

The Appreciative Inquiry Alternative I Envisioned

I continued to see power as an influence on how an organization engaged in diversity strategies and began to question the relationships. What emerged through my research and consultancies was the ability to identify groups of people who were the predominate recipients of organizational successes such as promotions, raises, and perks, display actions that suggested their feeling threatened if asked to share these organizational successes (Cross, 2000; Easley, 2001, 2002).

When this level of fear exists, individuals are neither going to be open to traditional methods of intervention, nor are they typically going to feel a kindred spirit with the individuals they perceive to be the threat. On the opposite side of the coin, those that feel disenfranchised have little to no motivation to go beyond the scope of their daily requirements.

Therefore, there was a distinct possibility that the traditional theoretical framework for investigating human action and interaction would not be appropriate when working to develop an organizational climate that valued the broad continuum of difference and unity of life. Was there a flaw in my logic at that juncture—respectfully,

I suggest no. However, there were limitations to my propositions, which I will address further along in the chapter.

Armed with this cognitive dissonance, I began to investigate how Appreciative Inquiry could both promote a deeper understanding of the organization's culture and invoke a different perspective regarding the hearts and souls of the people within the organization.

Appreciative Inquiry (AI) is an organization development intervention strategy, which has the ability to help organizational members focus on discovering, understanding, and fostering innovations in social organizational arrangements and processes (Cooperrider, 1986). AI includes a structured mode of inquiry where individuals can be inspired, mobilized, and moved on the road for sustaining human systems change. As a methodology, AI seeks to locate and heighten the "life-giving properties" or core values of organizations and the individuals within the organizations, which can move one's thinking beyond the boundaries of external difference (Cooperrider and Srivastva, 1987; Thatchenkery, 1996). AI also challenges the assumptions of traditional diversity interventions and training by actively seeking how organizations can engage in dialogue that is focused on the goal of seeking a common positive vision of a collectively desired future (Barrett and Cooperrider, 1990) versus starting with a problem solving orientation. Appreciative Inquiry or AI thus seeks out the very best of "what is" to provide an impetus for imaging "what might be" (Thatchenkery, 1996).

The four basic principles that are the foundation for AI include:

1. Inquiry into the "art of the possible" in individual or organizational life should begin with appreciation.
2. Inquiry into what's possible should be applicable.
3. Inquiry into what's possible should be provocative.
4. Inquiry into the human potential of organizational life should be collaborative (Cooperrider, 1986).

Therefore, within the context of AI's principles of possibility, application, provocation, and collaboration, questions surface. Consequently, I began exploring if AI would be able to successfully work as a diversity intervention strategy by facilitating an understanding of behavior within the organization from a different lens— the lens of positive interactions.

I also wanted to know if AI could move an organization from a compliance perspective toward one where an understanding of how to utilize difference to build organizational capacity would emerge, thereby bringing forth an ecumenical movement that would awaken the spirit to the unity of life.

The Opportunity to Implement My Propositions and Questions

Prior to presenting my work at the conference, I was asked to provide "diversity" training to approximately one thousand members within an organization in a three-month time period, which in and of itself was a huge task. This was the state organization previously referenced that was under consent decree, which resulted in a court-ordered mandate to engage in diversity training. Unfortunately, the organization and its leadership were very hostile to being forced to engage in this training. The consent decree was required because of the extensive claims that had been filed for both racial and gender biases. The claimants had won their cases and the result was the Equal Employment Opportunity Commission (EEOC) invoking its federally mandated privilege to "assist" the organization in addressing its issues.

We had 90 days to conduct this "training"—a mandate by the EEOC. I was also very concerned as to whether or not diversity training would even work in this organization and tried to walk away from the consult. However, because this organization was a sister state organization, a colleague and I were asked by the president of my university to embark upon this challenge. Since walking away from the consult would be "problematic," I decided to design a training program that would engage the organization in AI, which would serve as both a mechanism for delivering training as well as a way in which to hopefully get the organization moving toward capacity building versus focusing on its problems with difference (Easley, 2002).

The proposal for the training design was submitted to the agency's Equal Employment Opportunity (EEO) group. In the proposal, I submitted the proposition that a positive orientation toward examining diversity issues within the organization could help move both employees and managers into an interactive process where they could begin to understand, through inquiry, where their common visions were, relative to diversity within their respective departments, and where their strengths may already lie relative to managing diversity. Through structured inquiry, they would also be tasked within the context of the inquiry to search for solutions, which would facilitate their movement by focusing on the positive forces that already existed and the development of action plans to build upon these positive forces (Easley, 2002). Inclusively, through the structured inquiry, the managers would not be positioned to view themselves, their management styles, or their departments from a negative deficient orientation, which they felt was perceived as the catalyst for this court degree (Easley, 2002).

Additionally, through positive dialogue in a dialogical environment where the interveners (e.g. trainers) would not entertain negative images, the seed would be planted as to how both managers and employees could begin to understand the barriers that surrounded the acceptance of difference. Inclusively, employees and managers could begin, through a visioning process inherent in the AI, to see how they could individually and organizationally challenge and work through existing barriers, thus facilitating an organization-wide approach to ameliorating any discrimination issues that might be working within the organization (Easley, 2002).

Augmenting the foundational principles of AI is the postmodern organization development theory that frames how inquiry into organizational structures calls for the study of organizations as evolving, transforming, social constructions and malleable to human choice (Barrett and Srivastva, 1991). It was believed that by taking the organization through an inquiry (which was not going to be an easy answer to the court decree), where choices and patterns of interaction were examined within the context of appreciation, a seed would be planted in the employees, which would facilitate their movement toward transforming their behavior.

Unfortunately, the irony of this organization was that they did not see themselves as having a diversity problem—a direct result of how ingrained they were in their behavior, which also was predicated upon fear since many of the positions in the organization (both staff and management) were special appointments (Easley, 2002).

It was at this point that I began to better understand the issues of power and influence and their relationship to diversity—information that I have never forgotten. When lecturing on the topic of diversity to my students—even today—I respectfully submit to them that before they identify an organization and/or group of individuals as "racist," "prejudiced," "gender-biased," or afflicted with any other "ism" they wish to attribute, they should look at both the spoken and the unspoken dynamics and perspectives associated with power—a point to which I will return from time to time throughout this book.

The Intervention

The structure of the program introduced the concept of diversity via film and a very brief presentation on the demographic trends in their environment. However the bulk of the session was devoted to the AI intervention. Both management and employees dialogued on the following questions and then later shared their feedback with the larger group. More important than the specifics of their answers was their deconstructing of the learning that they gleaned from their interactions, which were grounded in a positive dialogical environment.

a. Without being humble, talk about what you value most about yourself, as a human being, a friend, and a member of this organization. What do you feel is the most valuable thing you have done within your community and organization toward furthering the concept of valuing diversity?

b. What was one of the best or most rewarding times working as a manager/employee within _____? Talk about the time that was a real high point and you felt most alive, most proud to be you and valued yourself the most. What made it a high point in your life? Who were the significant people that were part of this experience and why were they significant? What skills did you see yourself exhibit?

c. Building upon the information that we have covered today, talk about the diverse group of employees you have had in your various experiences as a manager/employee within _____, and what has impacted you the most about those individuals. What were the strengths you saw in those employees/colleagues? How did they contribute to the organizational goals and how did you help them build capacity? When did you feel most alive working with this diverse group and what made it a high point in your experience as a manager/employee?

d. If you could look to the future and use Appreciative Inquiry to add just one thing to your department to enhance diversity and begin to mend the misunderstandings that tend to arise out of differences in order to help your employees/colleagues feel valued more and hopeful, what would that be? How would you begin to think about building upon your personal strengths and the strengths you have talked about with the diverse people you have encountered within your organization? (Easley, 2002)

The last segment of the session focused upon a wrap-up, which was designed to focus on the next steps.

When the participants (that included both management and staff) were asked what they saw as the strengths of using an appreciative process toward understanding diversity, a representative sampling of their responses were as follows:

1. This training program was much less confrontational and that made it a lot easier to openly discuss differences.
2. Learning how to get along.
3. In using an appreciation process, you could better understand the other person's perspective in work and life.
4. The appreciative process avoided defensive responses, thereby promoting change.
5. Gave a different perspective on addressing diversity in an organization.
6. Self-acceptance; focus of personal weaknesses as well as strengths.
7. You can't make any improvements by focusing on negatives. Improvements can only be made and measured in a positive direction.
8. It focuses on the positive contribution of the individual while respecting cultural difference. It brings the cultural difference to the forefront, raising sensitivity.
9. Building on strengths rather than focusing on "Problems." Good approach.
10. Less stressful, accomplish more. (Easley, 2002)

While the utilization of AI as a diversity intervention/training session was successful, it still only provided a very quick fix strategy to a burning problem. What also emerged from examining this work environment were very deeply imbedded issues of power and control that emanated from the workers as well as the leadership. There were also significant issues of gender bias. Women were not routinely hired into this organization and the few that were expressed issues that ran along the continuum of not having proper areas to dress to experiencing significant sexual harassment by the men. The workforce did not fear reprisal from management, which may have been why there were so many EEOC claims that led to this consent decree. And, while the outcome of the dialogue ensconced in an appreciative context suggest opportunities for change—clearly the need for true change resided in the organization's leadership taking the situation seriously in concert with importing into the organization's guiding values a strong belief in equality.

I also questioned what was it in the AI process that started to change the dialogue of this organization. You see, when a consent decree is levied, it is the judicial system's way of expressing a belief that an organization is incapable of voluntarily complying with change (Easley, 2002).

At some level, the application of AI helped this organization visualize positive imagery, which helped the organization to begin to awaken to its own self-healing powers (Cooperrider, 1986). Yet, in the back of my mind, I knew it would be short-lived without the other aforementioned additions. Leaders have to set the stage that they are driving a culture change, and more importantly, they have to be willing to invest the time in the change processes.

The organization complied with the consent decree—period. The dissonance I felt was when I examined the individual relationships within the workforce. Interestingly, despite cultural, ethnic, and gender differences, I saw and heard individuals who on another spectrum generally had good intentions with respect to their interactions with one another from a one-on-one perspective (Easley, 2002). They just did not know how to translate their individual interactions to a collective consciousness that valued the organization's humanity. Consequently, they abdicated to confrontations as their primary method of interacting with one another (Easley, 2002).

The fact that the members could not view their circumstances from a negative deficient orientation or "solve" their problems helped prompt a more open dialogue. Yet, I still believe that people feared what they did not understand, and they did not understand at its basic root how to value difference. Consequently, when you augment the power and influence issues, particularly with appointed positions and people lackeying for favoritism, the situation, which was already complex, became even more complicated.

Although short-lived, the positive side of the AI interaction was in asking participants to simply talk about the goodness within themselves, their relationships and their environment—in other words, embrace their humanity. You could see the dynamics between individuals shift during the inquiry. Equally important, when asked to envision how they would want a changed environment to look, they could.

During the training, I also observed that when they engaged in a value-based conversation, they began to re-story their accomplishments from a different social context, which was not ensconced in an "us versus them" venue. Through AI, they were asked to challenge their concepts of race juxtaposed against their interpersonal interactions with their colleagues, which began to facilitate an examination of the ideals they held and what they believed society held relative to difference, in contrast to their daily relationships (Easley, 2002).

While there were clear dichotomies between their societal beliefs and their "real" interactions, the outcomes of their dialogues suggested that an environment that did not facilitate the need for defensive behaviors was clearly a preferred choice for reconciling any cognitive dissonance that may have surfaced with a diversity dialogue (Easley, 2002).

Overall, the employees did not want the discord that ran rampant through the organization. However, promoting change required guidance from the top of the organization. I believe that if we had a longer period of time to work with the workers and their respective leadership and management teams, there would have been an opportunity to evoke sustaining change. Their initial responses indeed suggested the planting of a seed of change where they "humanized" the concept of and constructs associated with diversity (Easley 2002).

The outcome of three months of training firmly rooted my belief that the downside to many diversity intervention strategies, howsoever creative they may have been in their design, was the fact that these strategies still tended to resemble structural design processes, which miss the human element in change initiatives. Changing the way an organization values humanity requires more time than leaders generally want to give to a change process. And, the leadership has to envision and import throughout the organization an appreciation for difference (Easley, 2002).

Without this level of engagement and follow-up, I suspect these efforts were short-lived. It was not part of our charge to longitudinally examine the organization—we were simply there to help them comply with a regulatory agency. This experience left me wondering how many organizations experienced similar limitations with their "change" strategies and only invoke diversity training and/or interventions to mark off an annual task.

Movement Toward Another Level of Understanding

In 2003, a journal article Dr. Alvarez and I wrote, published in the *Organization Development Journal*, continued to challenge many praxes regarding both diversity strategies and qualitative interventions. Our cognitive dissonance with where we were continued, and our concerns were basic and were based upon the proposition that *workers* were (and still are from a contemporary viewpoint) in the modality of redefining their expectations of the workplace. In other words, while employers have high expectations of their workforce, many literature streams heavily focus on the disconnects employees feel from their workplace, the organizational impact of those disconnects, and how employees desire a stronger connection to their place of work in order to feel validated in their contributions and worth to the organization's mission, values, and goals.

It will take an individual with extremely strong faith, personality, intestinal fortitude, and focus to move beyond a feeling of being devalued in an organization.

Yet, if leaders were cognizant of their work environment, and the feelings that their people may have, again at that visceral level I have previously referenced, many of the organizational stressors, such as high absenteeism, turnover, and so on could be significantly eliminated. Organizational leaders have to understand that no matter how much they perceive themselves in control, when you fail to validate the humanity of your workers, your organization will lose. So, while I am never comfortable in making a business case for experiencing the transcendence of all human life, there clearly are financial impacts when organizations fail to do so.

Turnover is very costly and recruiting processes are very expensive. When organizations lose employees, they also lose productivity because of a need to replace people. The learning curve that ensues once new employees are hired is typically very costly (Robinson-Easley, 2013). High levels of absenteeism cost, because the organization is forced to either run overtime and/or lose output by virtue of the absence (Robinson-Easley, 2013).

When stressed, employees tend to incur high medical bills due to the stress they are internalizing because they feel such a high level of cognitive dissonance working in an environment where they feel "less than," thereby driving up the cost of the organization's medical insurance (Robinson-Easley, 2013). And, the organization may risk more accidents in the organization due to employee burnout and fatigue, thereby increasing workers' compensation costs.

There are many more negative financial impacts—I am naming just a few. There are also the intangible impacts such as a poor external reputation, which ultimately impacts the organization's brand and resulting competitive advantage (Robinson-Easley, 2013). In other words, your organization will definitely not make the list of the top 100 places to work!!!

Human resource policies influence employee decisions about staying with the organization as well as joining the organization. Many employees, even in economic downturns will look to join organizations that appear to match their needs (Bellou, 2007). Consequently, human resource policies are critical elements in the formation of psychological contracts (2007).

So what does this mean relative to diversity issues? There is indeed a dualistic relationship; human resource policies (for example what really constitutes an egalitarian environment in an organization) affect the formation of psychological contracts. Consequently, if the organization has policies (and, equally important, actions) that send members positive signals relative to the relationship, then the organization can experience high levels of job satisfaction, commitment, and loyalty (2007). Yet, if employees believe that the organization has breached its respective psychological contract(s), employees may engage in counterproductive behaviors (2007), which definitely will impact the organization's bottom line.

In a recent study in the United Kingdom that incorporated quantitative and qualitative research methods, human resource professionals were interviewed regarding their human capital value creation strategies and resulting disclosures. The organizations reported how employee skills, education commitment, positive attitudes and behaviors, in concert with motivation are considered to be contributors to value creation (Beattie and Smith, 2010). Additionally, the study found employers capturing information on turnover, training and development, workplace safety, employee satisfaction, motivation, and commitment (2010).

Yet, some suggest that the number of organizations that engage in measuring human capital issues may be small for a variety of reasons that include the inability of human resource executives to point to data that synchs with the business programs and the value of human resource programmatic initiatives (Cantrell, Benton, Laudal, and Thomas, 2006).

Therefore, if both the organization's leadership and human resource teams do not understand the relational aspects of valuing the humanity of their workforce, they risk incurring negative economic impact to the organization's bottom line.

Issues of burnout have become so widespread in organizations that people continue to search for meaning and purpose to their lives. As a result, people are quite comfortable with challenging the mere acquisition of material gains and status, which tend to no longer satisfy a fulfillment. Juxtaposed to these propositions, today's workforce wants to make a difference by creating meaningful work and living with integrity that is embodied with an element of sacredness in their relationships.

They want to be able to positively impact their organizations by transforming them into communities where *everyone* benefits (Harmon and Hormann, 1990). However, most important, they want to move away from the cold, hostile, and demanding environments that tend to characterize the workplace, which is eroding their souls—an environment that tends to exist when organizations fail to recognize the human side of work (Maslach and Leiter, 1997).

Unfortunately, as people search for meaning in their lives and seek to deepen their organizational relationships, their organizations are more than ever depersonalizing their relationships with their workers, often resulting in a denigration in values, dignity, spirit, and will, a malady that spreads gradually and continuously over time, putting people in an organization into a downward spiral from which it is hard to recover (Maslach and Leiter, 1997), (Easley and Alvarez-Pompilius, 2003).

Many workers in today's globally challenging environment are being encouraged to better understand themselves via viewing and understanding their ontologies, epistemologies, and hermeneutics in order to construct their new place in today's global economy. This simply means that the organization's leaders as well as workforce should, from an ongoing mindset, restructure old personal belief systems (Robinson-Easley, 2013) that move away from identifying workers in descriptive ways that depict only a monetary value to their service. When valued, workers have the ability to move beyond the status of producers of widgets and digits and/or service and serve as the heart and soul of the organization. Yet, we continue to have such a reductionist view toward the people who are in actuality, despite all the automation one wants to place within the organization, the real producers.

This was clearly the case at the state agency I had worked with that was under the consent decree. You see, their legal issues did not just reside in their having to comply with a consent decree. State agencies across the country were being challenged to move toward privatization in an effort to reduce costs. Therefore, the old, yet prevailing paradigm of not needing to change due to their being invincible was rapidly becoming outdated. As a result, the old prevailing paradigm of invincibility on the part of the workforce was rapidly losing strength and position.

However, what the leadership of the organization appeared to not understand were the consequences associated with their failure to respect the human dignity of their coworkers, and hold their employees accountable for that same level of respect. There clearly was a bigger picture to factor in and that was a rapidly declining state budget. Unwarranted costs such as senseless litigation could no longer be tolerated.

Connecting the Lessons

From the lens of organization development, the strategies I described in my work were, in many venues, considered state of the art. For example, AI is an extremely popular and worldwide used organization development intervention. Yet, while the immediate impact was felt, the critique of how sustainable training is in any form or fashion was present, even in the venue of AI. In this particular case, AI was the lesser of the training and intervention "evils" because of its previously described attributes. However, those attributes could not overshadow what was needed from the leadership of the organization.

Leaders have to be the organization's champion in insuring that their employees' humanity is valued. Leaders need to invest their personal energy and commitment to changing the organization's cultural and diversity environments in concert with a commitment to invest an appropriate amount of time to really work toward sustainable change.

I learned that diversity strategies should not be solely championed and driven from mid-level management. If a diversity vision does not resonate and come from the leadership of the organization, a leadership prepared to make the critical humanistic connections and business case for valuing difference, the organization might as well throw their investment of money and time toward something else.

So, the real question that remains at this point is, how should these issues be addressed?

Chapter Four

The Importance of the Individual When Working to Evoke a Diverse Organizational Environment

It is very possible that the leadership of an organization might balk at the thought of including workers in the conversation regarding the process of analyzing and developing diversity strategies. Yet, who better knows what they need?

While organizations are evolving, transforming social constructions that are also malleable to human choice (Barrett and Srivastva, 1991), human choice has many facets of influence. Friday and Friday (2003) quoting Williams and O'Reilly suggested that diversity refers to "any attribute that happens to be salient to an individual that makes him and her perceive that he/she is different from another individual" (Muhtada, 2012). Therefore, before attempting to change behavior, those seeking to either change or be changed should examine and understand the human choices that they make and the underlying premises for those choices (Barrett and Srivastva, 1991).

Muhtada (2012) begins an interesting discourse regarding this issue when exploring diversity from a Muslim context. Far too often we want to place people along a singular continuum with the expectation that they can and will be able to come on board with any different type of change initiative. Citing the varying areas of the Quran that speak to the issue of valuing difference, Muhtada suggested that because there is a continuum along which Muslims feel comfortable with diversity management as it pertains to women and non-Muslim leadership, there is a need to incorporate an understanding of this continuum and prevailing belief systems around issues of gender equity into their organizational change strategies (2012).

Therefore, another example of the often unexplored salient points of microcultural differences and potential impact upon diversity management are the microcultural differences of pluralism and multiculturalism values in Islamic teaching, which may be significant starting areas for developing a diversity management discourse and set of strategies in the Muslim community context (Muhtada, 2012).

In practice, I saw Muhtada's propositions in a health care setting. There were many issues between the nursing staff, which was primarily African American, and the physician staff that was primarily Indian and African physicians with a smaller representation of African American doctors. However, when addressing issues of diversity and strategies that were needed to better the working relationships between the nursing and the physician staff, the president at that time could not "see" issues of diversity because in his mind the staff was comprised of people of color—so what could possibly be a diversity issue?

When I gently explained to him the microcultural issues just around the concept of gender, he had great difficulty fathoming what these issues meant and how they could manifest in conflict. Yet, the communication breakdown between the nurses and physicians, unaddressed, was impacting patient satisfaction. It was not until the problems reached a disproportionate level was the president willing to thoroughly listen to this conversation and agree to the need for a dialogue that addressed diversity. He failed to understand that even when you have people from similar skin colors, their cultural as well as microcultural differences can and do play important roles in the organization. Unfortunately, it was not until the manifestation of these "roles" began to have a negative impact on the financials of the hospital was he ready to even entertain the possibilities—which made me wonder how many other leaders face similar blind spots. When healthcare providers fail to address diversity, there can be poor communication that creates many barriers between health care professionals and patients (Jimenez-Cook and Kleiner, 2005).

Organizations, and those involved in diversity research and management, should be highly sensitive to how people construct a one-dimensional narrative of the change process. Organizations should not want to have their leadership and management team portrayed as all-knowing rationalist masters; a phenomenon that can occur when a one-dimensional narrative is allowed to continue (Bissett, 2004). Organizations embody contradictions and confusion, which can and often do reduce the managerial responses to an "old times" rationalist modernist approach shrouded in similarly situated assumptions (Bissett, 2004).

Unfortunately, far too many organizations that have been researched yielded data that suggested that despite employees express-ing feelings of profound differentiation and fragmentation, their respective managers continued to assume a widespread uniformity of perspectives (Harris and Ogbonna, 1998, as cited in Bissett, 2004).

The late Gloria Anzaldúa similarly addressed the many dimen-sions of contradictions when examining the mestiza culture—critical lessons for organizations in as much as Hispanics now comprise a significant percentage of America's diversity.

Throughout my years in the corporate environment, I never heard of Anzaldúa's work, although when I did study her writing, I found her books to be critical contributions to the diversity con-versations. It was not until I went to seminary and studied global ministry that I came face to face with her research and writing—which is both groundbreaking and foundational to understanding many of the nuances of difference not only within Hispanic culture, but also indicative of issues that occur in other cultures. What sig-nificantly struck me were Anzaldúa's propositions on the relational issues between the mestiza and white America and their impact on the concept and construct of subjugation. Critically, she wrote

> The dominant white culture is killing us slowly with its ignorance. By taking away our self-determination, it has made us weak and empty. As a people we have resisted, and we have taken expedient positions, but we have never been allowed to develop unencumbered—we have never been allowed to be fully ourselves. The whites in power want us people of color to barricade ourselves behind our separate tribal walls so they can pick us off one at a time with their hidden weapons; so they can whitewash and distort history. Ignorance splits people, creates prejudices. A mis-informed people is a subjugated people (2007, p. 108).

While one may (as have others) categorize her points of view as radi-cal, I believe there are lessons we should draw from Anzaldúa's expe-riences and analyses that are germane to critically understanding people who do not comprise the dominate culture in any social context. Anzaldúa closely examined issues of walking a borderland of consciousness, which she saw as being marked by a plurality of personality that possesses psychic restlessness. Juxtaposed against this psychic restlessness was a conflict she observed between perceiving oneself as visible and concomitantly invisible because one has been forced to walk outside the boundaries of that which was originally your culture, a culture that was taken over, rendering you as the "other" (Anzaldúa 2007; Anzaldúa and Keating, 2002).

As I studied liberation theology, I often found the concept of *othering,* which I mentioned in the introduction, addressed by many theologians. The concept and construct of this word reminded me of concepts I would hear when engaging in diversity council sessions during my years in the corporate business sector. You see, the word *othering* is often used to connote difference and, when speaking of people who have different characteristics from those considered to be "mainstream," will incorporate sometimes subtle and not-so-subtle references that demonize and dehumanize groups that are "different," which for some (particularly when we are justifying the need to retain power and privilege) further justifies attempts to civilize and exploit these "inferior" others ("Other," The Free Dictionary).[1].

Yet, when we love ourselves and our humanity and extend the same to others, we soon learn. "While I know myself as a creation of God, I am also obligated to realize and remember that everyone else and everything else are also God's creation." Maya Angelou[2]

When we continue to operate in a context where people continue to fight for their rights to equal pay, jobs, promotions, and other aspects of the employment relationship, is it too far of a reach to think that people who feel devalued also feel "othered"? I often wonder if organizations actually factor into their balance sheets the economic impact of this "othering."

Even when we look at the need to retain power and position, I do not believe that it has to be an issue of putting one group or groups of people down in order to retain anything. While studies show the downside of not valuing diversity, there are many organizations that have prospered by embracing the humanity of their people and work to make them feel a part of the organization. So, in reality, the end results of valuing humanity can be a win-win situation. Those in power can retain and even enhance their "power" when they are surrounded by and working with people who know they are valued and will go above and beyond to take care of their work home. In other words, there truly is a value proposition that can be stated when a leader and his or her respective organization values their people and takes time to understand the nuances of their culture and microcultures. Equally important, this value proposition has staying power; the organizations that engage in the effort and time that it takes to value the humanity of their workforce can and do outlast their competition.

Maybe organizational leaders are not intentionally dehumanizing or forcing the psychic restlessness that Anzaldúa cites, but nevertheless there are far too many situations in which they exist. There is unwarranted stressfulness that exist in the lives of individuals when they have to daily come into a work environment in which they feel devalued—the pain of looking at people less qualified than them being moved ahead or making more money simply because an organizational leader or manager has decided to invoke his or her personal biases into employment decisions, even if the law may be very clear as to the illegality of these actions, or, equally devastating, an organization choosing to allow substandard work conditions to prevail simply because it is not their own cultural or business context. Far too often, when organizational leaders are geographically and culturally removed from the immediacy of a work environment, a detachment toward the plight of the people, their connection to humanity, and the particulars of their circumstances will prevail. Yet, there is hope that is embedded in Anzaldúa's proposed conclusions. As she respectfully stated—the mestiza endures and is able to cross over these invisible (and physical) barriers, and the mestiza evolves from this othering experience and emerges a stronger and a more malleable species, forced to embrace hybridity and flexibility, attributes that strengthen the character and will to survive (Anzaldúa, 2007). Many cultures endure and survive. The question, however, is, is this "survival" justified? Should not every person be allowed to flourish to his or her maximum capabilities without others putting them down?

Why, in today's environment, are we still imposing constraints that reside under the umbrella of disempowerment in an organization, yet still are adamant about designing and implementing "change strategies" to break through these barriers, only to have halfhearted initiatives backfire in the face of the organization? Why should people have to break through barriers in order to realize their strength? What is so difficult about understanding that when you fail to respect people and to treat them with dignity and respect, they will rebel in one form or another—whether it is low production, poor attitudes, sabotage, or a combination of varying actions? Anzaldúa also saw the counter-stance that the mestiza assumes as a step toward liberation (Anzaldúa, 2007; Anzaldúa and Keating, 2002). Friere saw it in the people of Brazil, his commentary spoke volumes:

> Liberation is thus a child birth, and a painful one. The man or woman who emerges is a new person, viable only as the oppressor-oppressed contradiction is superseded by the humanization of all people. Or to put it another way, the solution of this contradiction is born in the labor which brings into the world this new being: no longer oppressor no longer oppressed, but human in the process of achieving freedom. (Friere, 2006, p. 49)

When we take on a defiant "Hell no, I am not buying your attempts to marginalize me" attitude, I believe we are forced to come to grips with who we are and look internally to our strengths (Robinson-Easley, 2012). It is important that every member of the organization take a counter-stance—leaders, employees, country leaders, those that feel marginalized within their communities. The venue does not matter. Where there is a failure to respect difference is often an environment that risks eventually becoming paralyzed, either mentally or physically.

Interestingly, when I looked at some of the reviews of Anzaldúa's work, she was labeled as angry (Robinson-Easley, 2012). However, from my lens, Anzaldúa is not angry; she is speaking the truth from the lens of someone who faced discrimination. You see, it is not until you have had to face the "othering" process that you can truly understand feeling like your soul is being ripped apart. You have no choice but to walk away stronger, because the other options are not palatable or productive. This is why privileging one's lens is so important. You do not do justice to a situation when you always attempt to be neutrally positioned, albeit an objective viewpoint is critical to incorporate into the analyses—feelings, deep seated feelings are just as valid in understanding the critical roadblocks that can and do exist.

As I write this book, I also wonder if the people who really need to read it—those at the helm of our global organizations—will truly attempt to understand the nuances of my propositions; or will I, too, be labeled simply as an angry Black woman because I also take a counter-stance and offer a different paradigm? Has the ability to label an individual who challenges the prevailing paradigms become the norm for summarily dismissing perspectives that challenge individuals to morph their thinking to higher level of consciousness? Or, is Thurman's proposition on change a more appropriate stance:

> Always there is some voice that rises up against what is destructive, calling attention to an alternative, another way. It is a matter of more than passing significance that the racial memory as embodied in the myths of creation, as well as in the dream of prophet and seer, points ever to the intent to community as the purpose of life (Thurman, 1963, p. 94).

Labeling and unequal treatment, which are the foundational behaviors that keep the equal employment agencies in business, represent unsophisticated yet far too often bought-into *defense* mechanisms designed to maintain current balances of power. While I clearly understand the concept of power and influence, I also understand that if we make a conscious choice to invoke a humanitarian approach to people in our organizational environments, as I continue to respectfully suggest, we increase power and equality. More importantly, we build capacity through community, again pointing to how the dualistic concepts of difference and commonality can indeed reside in one domain.

The interesting outcome of what Anzaldúa brings to this contextual conversation, which parallels so many diverse people's experiences, is that out of anger we can emerge far more actualized than we were when we initially embarked upon crossing our own borders. Inherent in this emergence is also the flexibility that we develop because of our counter-stance to the rigidity of *definition* and superimposed attempts to place us where the dominate culture prefers for us to reside (Robinson-Easley, 2012). Yet, why do we have to go to these extremes?

The Complexity of an Individual

Diversity change should be grounded in both epistemological and ontological reasoning, which is why I believe it critical that the propositions within this book are contextually framed to position the reader to examine the concept and context of diversity from lens of color.

You see, before you can buy into a change proposal that incorporates the dynamics articulated in this book, the reader has to *personally* resonate with it.

Let us go back and revisit Pettigrew's propositions. Simply stated, Pettigrew (1979) suggested that when we openly acknowledge our personal qualities and experiences, we also open space for another level of a consciousness of meaning to enter that can be subtle yet of significant impact when deconstructing how we create and manage sense and meaning (Pettigrew, 1979). This perspective is critical for both the worker and the organizational leaders if they are to truly move beyond the surface when looking to insure that they have an organizational environment that values difference.

When we understand how we choose to view the world and its respective actors from our epistemological and ontological grounding, we also begin to understand our choices with respect to how we interact with people. We may not like our ontological context— many great leaders have chosen to move beyond their history, upbringing, and resulting psychological contexts and perspectives. Yet, these are critical insights for organizational leaders as well as workers—each possessing clear choices as to how they champion their right to be different. Let me return to the example of my seminary colleagues. While I saw members of this community, who also comprised the LGBT community, ask tough questions regarding their relationships with their Creator and their right to make their personal choices—questions that would have broken the spirits of other people, I also saw them emerge as much stronger individuals—strength that was clearly going to be needed as they ministered to other people who spiritually and theologically would be facing their own brokenness.

Leaders should work to understand *their* ontology and how it informs their perspectives on power, privilege, difference, and equally important issues of compliance. As a result, when one understands the complexity of their personal ontology, perhaps they can become more sensitized to the complexity of individuals and not work to loosely categorize them in buckets of ethnicity, race, gender, or other categories. I respectfully suggest to global leaders that while this type of introspective analysis may not be comfortable, it is necessary in today's global environment to move their organizations, the people who work for those organizations, and, equally important, themselves, to a new level. We have already established the context that our world is constantly changing—yet what we often do not do is embrace the really important strategies that are important to evoke the change that is necessary to keep up with the rapidity of our evolution.

We have the ability to intentionally move our understanding and knowledge of how we view difference beyond surface levels to a much deeper sense of understanding as to how we relate to our internal and external worlds, which can lead to a clearer understanding of how we categorize the many layers of self that give rise to our resulting hermeneutics.

How do people "know," and is "knowing" important when looking to value difference in any context—organizational, community, and so on? I find it interesting, yet vastly appropriate that Muhtada's point of reference when examining diversity within a Muslim context is the Holy Quran, which speaks to integrating roles and responsibilities from cultural and theological contexts. He further posits that human resource strategies that are geared to address diversity should incorporate Muslim scholars who understand Islamic values of pluralism and multiculturalism *and* are also familiar with human resource managerial skills (2012). If Anzaldúa were living, I believe if asked what would be her recommendations regarding diversity initiatives she might posit similar sentiments.

My research has led me to other African American scholars who also suggest that the traditional ways of helping a community of people invoke a deep discursive understanding of self, change, and difference is insufficient. Many African American scholars continue to search for alternative ways of helping our people engage in effective "knowing." When we know, we can better work toward change (Easley, 2010).

For example, the emergence of Black psychology represents a counter way of looking at African Americans by deconstructing a worldview that is believed to intentionally rob most members of the human family of their divinely given right to know and define their humanity in the context of their legacy and particular cultural experience (Akbar, 2003). Similar to the experiences of people who live in the French West Indies, our historical context is very important to understanding how African Americans view our world.

Black theology, a form of liberation theology, came explicitly out of the social and political trauma of the 1960s and is said to represent a socially located form of theological reflection. The construct of Black theology entails Black people's reflection on the Black experience while seeking to articulate the historic effects of racism on the lives and psyches of dark-skinned people (Brown, 2004).

Within a similar time frame, womanist theology emerged as a counter to feminism. Black female scholars suggest that feminism in general, and Christian feminism in particular, had been developed by Caucasian women, with their histories, and limited the relevance of feminism for Black women in the United States, who have different experiences of domination. The hermeneutical approach that forms womanist interpretations is very contextual and begins with the social location of the Black woman (Brown, 2004; Mitchem, 2002). Yet, we cannot discount that the antecedents that impact our social location are also evolving—realities that should also be incorporated into helping African American women understand how we engage in sensemaking.

At the Core of the Issues Lies the Complex Core of the "Individual"

At the core of change, particularly when building an organization that truly values difference—globally or domestically—you are working with people and their varying ranges of differences that defy relegating them to a reductionist perspective. Understanding your people and their perspectives that frame their respective ways of knowing is critical when looking to evoke any type of organizational change—especially initiatives that are designed to build upon the beauty of difference.

How people choose to view others provides critical information regarding their core values. How the workforce views disempowerment is as critical. How the workforce views perceived change is foundational to insuring that you are addressing critical core strategies. Yet, the organization that does not take the time to examine and understand their workforce from a deep and personal level is risking spending a lot of time and money on change strategies that may ultimately result in either complete failure or a very short-term change.

The literature across many domains continues to bring forth challenges to the more traditionalized views of difference and its relationships to organizational theory. For example, an underlying premise of *recent* feminist thinking, in the post-structuralist context is taking an affirmative view of individuals existing in a *state of multiples* (Styhre and Eriksson-Zetterquist, 2008), propositions that are not too dissimilar from those in the womanist theological literature.

Subjectivities and identities are viewed as existing in multiple rather than singular form, diverse rather than unified and self-enclosed. Subject-positions are not viewed as fixed and unified but as fleeting and fluid identities that emerge in continuously changing networks of humans, technologies, and artifacts (Styhre and Eriksson-Zetterquist, 2008).

For example, utilizing these propositions, one can suggest that the oppression of women will vary upon a range of factors that include race, gender, class, culture, nationality, ethnicity, age, sexuality, disability, and reproductive status (Hutchinson and Mann, 2006, as cited in Styhre and Eriksson-Zetterquist, 2008). Consequently, rather than look at the singular concept of oppressing women, third-wave feminism examines what is multiple, which integrates various regimes of knowledge/power than impacts and/or determines women's social positions and opportunities for social action (Styhre and Eriksson-Zetterquist, 2008). Augmenting this perspective, the concept of intersectionality, first coined by Crenshaw (1990, 1994, as cited in Styhre and Eriksson-Zetterquist, 2008), was used to denote how Black women are exposed to a number of different regimes of discipline and oppression, where each will operate within its own conceptual category (Styhre and Eriksson-Zetterquist, 2008).

Similar in context to the praxes of womanist theology, Crenshaw suggested that it was the failure of the feminist literature to interrogate race and its inability to recognize the subordination of people of color that demanded a review of the relationship between systems of oppression (Styhre and Eriksson-Zetterquist, 2008). So, what can these propositions mean in an organizational context—simply the hiring of women who are both of color and/or Caucasian may not be the total answer to an organizational environment that does not suggest equality. For example,

> A unidimensional understanding of inequality breaks down with an intersectional lens. For instance, radical feminist claims that men oppress women miss the potential complexity of the economic relations between some groups of men and White women. In many cities, White women earn more than Black, Mexican-origin, and Puerto-Rican men. (Brown and Misera, 2003, p. 489, as cited in Styhre and Eriksson-Zetterquist, 2008)

Yet, when we incorporate an understanding of the complexity of the individual in organizational change strategies, different results begin to emerge. For example, in one study, 35 top corporate executives described the expression and demonstration of love for members of their organization, which in turn worked to encourage those organizational members to love one another, as key attributes for navigating the white waters of permanent change in the environment that was being studied (Vaill, 1996). It is plausible to then say that when we view people from a lens of love, we also open our ability to view their humanity from a very different lens; or as poignantly stated, "Where there is love there is no darkness" (Burundi Proverb).[3]

Should we then suggest that the foundational praxes of organizational spirituality, when building hopeful organizations that are built upon a sacred value for life, are far more critical diversity initiatives than traditional strategies? When looking to effect this level of transcendence, should organizations move toward an organizational movement that brings forth widespread inner spiritual awakening to the *unity of life* and consciousness? (Korten, 2001). Or are we destined to continue to exist in a mindset that continues to evoke criticism? Will the dominate Western tradition of thinking—its ontology and epistemology steeped by the thinking of philosophers such as Plato, Descartes, and Kant—continue to exist in a state where it readily falls victim to being accused of pursuing a reductionist mode of thinking (Styhre and Eriksson-Zetterquist, 2008, p. 577)?

Postmodern change theories have suggested for quite some time that societies should move away from focusing on weaknesses and our failure to understand the basic components that drive human nature (Easley and Swain, 2003; Ludema, 1996). Working to strengthen our collective capacity to imagine and build a better future infers working from a lens of value for our humanity. An equally meritorious proposition is that perhaps we also need to better understand the intersectionalist view of diversity, which will require unpacking and defamiliarizing the diversity concept as we now view it (Styhre and Eriksson-Zetterquist, 2008). Unpacking and defamiliarizing old concepts can bring forth cognitive dissonance. Yet, when we learn to value the unity of life, we concomitantly privilege its individuality.

In today's world, we have learned to become proficient problem solvers, and yet we continue to fail in engaging the life-giving dimensions of our organizations and employees, where we have a chance to more productively stimulate our action and thereby contribute to the growing development of human hope (Ludema, 1996). Yet, human hope is so needed in today's world of chaos. With people across the world expressing in many forms of communication, discontent with their present lives and environment, we have to work hard to keep the hope factor from diminishing. That is not to say that we are going to get things "right" the first time we invoke new paradigms, but I truly believe when organizations and their respective leaders are viewed as trying, people will gather together to move the train of hope and the resulting change actions forward. This potential growing development of human hope has the ability to serve as the conceptual lens for understanding and discovering the forces and factors that enhance human relatedness, while offering a collective sense of purpose (Ludema, 1996).

So, rather than suppress people when they rise up and express their discontents, we need new lens and strategies for engaging in productive discourse that will allow sacred space for all voices to be productively heard. Therefore, if we revisit Anzaldúa's propositions, is it fair to suggest that a better way exists to help the mestiza successfully navigate their borderlands than having to grow stronger out of a *struggle* with adversity? And when doing so, is it fair to suggest that we then strengthen our *collective* value propositions, which in the end results in increased capacity and power for all?

Unfortunately, in today's times, most people in public and private organizations are typically left out of the change strategies that are designed, developed, and implemented on their behalf (Swain, 1997). Consequently, we continue to implement new change programs that are contextually designed within the parameters of our newest theoretical principles that utilize traditional inquiry methods to evaluate their effectiveness, the soundness of which can be epistemologically questioned, while simultaneously failing to *involve* the people in the design and implementation of these programs (Claerbaut, 1983; Ludema, Wilmot, and Srivastva, 1997, p. 1018; Easley and Swain, 2003). People's voices need to be heard in an environment that encourages self and collective reflection. Let us again revisit Moltmann's proposition, which bears repeating:

> The way of political hermeneutics cannot go one-sidedly from reflection to action. That would be pure idealism. The resulting action would become blind. Instead, this hermeneutic must bind reflection and action together thus requiring reflection in the action as well as action in the reflection. The hermeneutical method to which this leads is called in the "ecumenical discussion" the action-reflection method. (Moltmann, 2006, p. 44)

And please do not allow his reference to the concept of ecumenical impede your understanding. A critical definition of the term ecumenical when used as an adjective is "of worldwide scope or applicability; universal."[4]

A failure to understand should be broken into manageable pieces, which allows people to directly engage in a discussion that is also embodied in a reflective and spiritual awareness (Korten, 2001) that empowers them to feel free to engage in discourse regarding their differences as well as common organizational visions and goals. This proposition would hold true whether we address a traditional organization, community, country, or any other type of context that binds people together.

Participants should be moved to begin the process of understanding the *unity* of life, which requires individuals working at a deeper personal and spiritual level when attempting to understand and appreciate difference (Korten, 2001; Easley, 2001).

Let us revisit my propositions in the abstract of my 2001 article, in today's (12 years later) context.

> Because the new millennium is bringing far greater diversity challenges to organizations, leaders will have to question their assumptions about past diversity initiatives and examine alternative change processes that incorporate the true instruments of change ... the people who work in the organizations. Therefore, this work begins a discussion, which

suggests a very different paradigm for moving an organization towards developing, valuing and managing diversity within this new millennium, while simultaneously examining the limitations of the more popular, but traditional diversity initiatives." (Easley, 2001, p. 39)

How does one embark upon the path for understanding the unity of life? The theoretical principles associated with sensemaking can serve as one point of reference, and in many ways complement the previously cited literatures (Black Psychology, Womanist Theology, etc.). When we begin to deconstruct our own ability to understand the unity of life, we cannot walk away from the notion of self, which is constantly refined by how we interpret our environment. Sensemaking is truly an iterative process that continually redesigns our image of self (Parry, 2003).

As a result, people and organizations produce or construct the environment they face. "They act and in doing so create the materials that become the constraints and opportunities they face" (Weick, 1995, p. 31, as cited in Parry, 2003). This then is the active part of the construction of reality—our sensemaking. Yet, we continually look back at our experience to make sense of what took place then, in the context of what we know and perceive now (2003). The danger with this reference point is that we may not factor in the ongoing expansive landscape of a global environment and the continually growing microcultures that are a critical part of today's global workforce. Retrospection often implies 20:20 hindsight, as Starbuck and Milliken (1988, pp. 37–40, as cited in Parry, 2003) have shown (2003). Executives may assume that errors of the past could have been avoided by more attention to process (2003).

However, should *process* be the real focus—or should we better understand the *social aspects* of sensemaking that are primarily constructed by networks of shared meaning? And, when working toward "shared meaning," should there be an intentional focus to avoid falling into the trap of power and the plausible imbalance in how our voices are "heard" and influenced? As Coopey et al, (1997) and Brown (1999), as cited in Parry, 2003) noted, not all voices are equal (Parry, 2003).

The awareness of a potential imbalance of power and how it can direct the discourse and resulting sensemaking may suggest a need for a new paradigm regarding power. Globally, alternative social practices that are rooted in alternative discourses are emerging. For example, the international Baha'i community, which includes over six million members, has suggested that contemporary world conditions are pressing humanity toward an age of global integration that will require new models of social organization and new levels of maturity in human interactions. And, they believe that this will require a rethinking of contemporary attitudes toward power (Baha'i World Centre, 2001, as cited in Karlberg, 2005). As this community grows in capacity and prominence, many of its structures and practices are attracting the attention of entities such as the United Nations. The United Nations and other outside observers recognize the potential of these paradigm shifts and resulting new systems as plausible systems that they might emulate (2005).

The Baha'i's alternative ways for thinking and talking about social power and social reality and the resulting systems are not the only models that suggest major shifts in paradigms regarding social change. Other faith communities, social movements, and nongovernmental organizations are also innovating new models of social change that *equalize* the playing fields (Karlberg, 2005).

Movement toward new paradigms for understanding difference and valuing humanity should incorporate an understanding that there is a deeper meaning to diversity and the individual that transcends our traditional understanding. The complexity of one is not to be feared. At the core of self, we have no choice but to understand the many layers it entails and there is a need to give those layers "voice."

A very important lesson that Dr. Alvarez and I learned was that in the midst of our many microcultural differences, we also possessed and learned to embrace our many similarities. Our differences and similarities, when simultaneously embraced, facilitated our growing strong as colleagues and friends. The positive outcome—everything we researched and wrote was either published and/or presented, nationally and internationally, which typically is an unusual academic record. More often than not, there will be some rejection rates. However, I attribute our success to our willingness to both embrace and understand our diversities at very deep discursive levels—never allowing our respective differences to become barriers to our goals and strategic foci regarding our research. Yet, other important behaviors emerged as important as we were learning to embrace our differences and similarities—we talked and listened to one another. We put into practice our respective training in sensemaking.

As Dr. Alvarez and I have moved forward with our current work in intercultural management, we also understand the intersectionality of our differences as well. You see, despite our common African lineage, the intersectionality of that lineage within our varying social contexts differently informs our view of intercultural management, which is a critical lens to helping others understand the vastness of this concept, and it calls for more conversations as we begin to expand our work through the book we are coediting.

Human beings are truly quite capable of self-directing their behaviors and possess the capacity to give meaning to their actions, when given the appropriate framework to explore change (Heron, 1971; Reason, 1988). Therefore, it is very important to engage organizational members in strategies that help *them* identify, assess, and understand their current behaviors, fears, and perceptions of limitation that may result when diversity changes are implemented that may in fact work to limit them and their ability to effectively perform at their "true" levels.

Involving people in a conversation that de-bundles the current organization's context of diversity and difference can give them sacred space to explore versus being told how to "resolve" their differences/diversities. In other words, this would encourage them as well as their leadership to explore how they make sense of their environment from a position of strength versus a deficit orientation that is clouded by feelings of being marginalized.

Consciously or not, when we attempt to locate people from diverse cultures and ethnicities in a uniformed place, we truly do risk confining their roles, thereby reducing the complexities of their lives to simple equations. We have to move past this reductionism perspective and seek effective ways to lift the souls of the people with whom we work. These lessons have not been easy ones to learn (Easley, 2010) but in today's continually changing global environment, I believe they become lessons that should be on the forefront of organizational leaders' agendas.

Chapter Five

Contemporary, Yet Unconventional Research and Perspectives on Issues of Diversity and Intercultural Management

The increasing pace of internationalization and the changing forms of globalization are requiring organizations to be very savvy in cross culturalism, particularly if they desire to position themselves for success. If an individual aspires to have a successful global career, cross-cultural competencies are absolutely necessary (Morley and Cerdin, 2010). Yet, there are still questions as to why some individuals have very little problems navigating cross-cultural experiences versus others who struggle with the competency (Morley and Cerdin, 2010).

In 2010, Wang and Mattila addressed the complexities of intercultural service encounters, attributing the difficulties of these experiences to both intergroup and interpersonal facets (Giles and Coupland, 1991, as cited in Wang and Matilla, 2010). Recent studies suggest that the racial differences between service providers versus the client are one of the major contributors to service breakdowns (Wang and Matilla, 2010).

Barker et al. (2008, as cited in Wang and Matilla, 2010) conducted a study that showed how African American customers are likely to attribute service failures to racial discrimination when they encounter white servers. Equally interesting, even when there is no service failure, intercultural service encounters tend to adversely affect the level of comfort with the service provider (Paswan and Ganesh, 2005, as cited in Wang and Matilla, 2010).

Barker and Hartel (2004) found that aboriginals and immigrants in Australia tended to feel unfriendliness, embarrassment, and ignored when interacting with local Australian service providers. Moreover, they also found the customers lacking a sense of trust and unwillingness to even interact with the servers (Wang and Matilla, 2010).

Yet, when reading this literature, I cannot help but continue to ask the question—are we discussing intercultural issues or are these findings grounded in issues that connote a failure to value difference, for example diversity?

When examining the sociocultural dimensions of management one should consider that social-cultural situations and developments, such as customs, habits, and codes of conduct have an enormous normative influence on human behavior (Neuert, Opel, and Schaupp, 2002). But is that any different when an organization functions within the United States and is working with people from various cultural, ethnic, and/or racial backgrounds and is servicing diverse communities? Are we continuing to blur lines that may not have as many differences as we envision?

I totally agree with the proposition that if not educated in the cultural context of the host country, business representatives can make major mistakes and sometimes those mistakes can negatively impact a business transaction. However, what continues to concern me is that we attribute cultural conflicts to primarily a lack of education. Are our failures to effectively function in an intercultural context truly reflective of our miseducation with respect to the culture or our failure to first and foremost understand that difference outside our domain does exist and we should learn to value the uniqueness of cultures and be savvy enough to question the appropriateness of our behaviors?

As I have traveled across many countries, I have found many perspectives regarding the arrogance of Americans. At first I was a bit taken aback, but until I began to step back and examine, when traveling in groups with people from the United States, the arrogance of our behaviors, I no longer could question why we so often can and will face disdain.

Bjerregaard, Lauring, and Anders (2009) cited research that argued how cross-cultural management is still entrenched in a functionalist or positivist paradigm with little reflection of the consequences. With supporting evidence from researchers such as Adler (1983), Boyacigiller and Adler (1991), Redding (1994), Sullivan (1998), Westwood (2001, 2004), and Whitley 1991, 1999, as cited in Bjerregaard et al., 2009), they warned that the theoretical understanding of culture that underlies these perspectives is based on a conception of culture as something self-contained and stable that can be identified and generalized (2009). Yet, one can also suggest that culture, when described in functionalist terms tends to become a static and decontextualized concept of little use when analyzing actual intercultural encounters (Saderberg and Holden, 2002, Vaara et al., 2003, as cited in Bjerregaard et al., 2009).

New perspectives, which are derived from many diverse epistemological positions, draw from postcolonial discourse analysis, Chicago school symbolic interactionism, semiotics, socially situated cognitivism, and phenomenology, and critically view the "culture fit" as an insufficient definition of the interplays between culture and agency, process, interests, and motives (Bjerregaard et al., 2009).

More specifically,

> These different streams of research have made various contributions in opening up the field for more multifaceted and context-sensitive understandings of culture in cross-cultural management (CCM). Phenomenological views in the CCM literature often draw on Weick's (1995) ideas about sensemaking as being socially situated in a local organizational context. Socially situated cognitivism is informed by anthropological research on cognition as socially distributed among organizational participants. Thereby, workplace dynamics are viewed as an integral part of culture. (Bjerregaard et al., 2009, p. 3)

Therefore, when deconstructing intercultural communications, your analysis should incorporate the nexus of culture, actors, and the context of the communication (Bjerregaard et al., 2009).

The proposition to incorporate the nexus of the culture and actors is not new theory. The conversations around the continuum of culture, more specifically the interplay between individualism and collectivism emerged as early as the 1970s (Triandis, Chan, Bhawuk, Iwao, and Sinha, 1995). Collectivism and individualism were seen as cultural syndromes, reflecting shared attitudes, beliefs, categorizations, norms, roles, and values organized around a central theme among individuals who live in a specific geographic region (Triandis, 1993, as cited by Triandis, Chan, Bhawuk, Iwao, and Sinha, 1995). Yet, on the other end of the continuum resided individualism, which positions individuals as autonomous from groups (1995). Fast forwarding the previously cited work, if you incorporate the concept of microcultures you further delineated those constructs by incorporating the vast arrays of difference that lie even within the individual point on the continuum. In other words, the concept of culture and intercultural exchange is complicated, but only if one walks in with the presumption that there is a unique sameness that originates from their personal cultural context.

In the early 1990s, programs were designed to prepare people for international assignments as a process in which one needed to be oriented to the differences in social interactions between cultures (Bhawuk and Brislin, 2000). While these programs have been around for a while, so has the term and concept of culture shock, which described problems faced by people who traveled from one culture to another. Broadly categorized as the anxiety people incurred when moving to other cultures, not only were there descriptors associated with psychological discomforts, but physical manifestations were noted and believed to be a result of the discomfort people experienced when finding themselves in different cultural contexts (2000).

While over the years there has been an increase in research studies and resulting training and development on the topic of culture shock and one's ability to effectively navigate the domains of other cultures (2000), there still appears to be an undercurrent of superiority that appears to give birth to the "shock" when visiting other countries. Throughout the years as people have experienced culture shock, one can and should ask: Is it really the shock of seeing and accommodating a different environment, or is there an arrogance that gives rise to a belief system that there has to be this "sameness"? Hall debunked the proposition of sameness as it related to intercultural exchanges in 1966 by positing the argument that people from different cultures not only speak different languages but also inhabit different sensory worlds and create a different environment around them (Hall, 1966, as cited in Bhawuk and Brislin, 2000).

Therefore, it is hard to understand why someone would not expect to encounter difference. It is equally hard to understand why there would be resistance toward developing a mindset toward effectively learning about, but more importantly, respecting those differences. As I have traveled globally, I have personally witnessed bold displays by my American colleagues of what appeared to be perceived social and economic superiority by virtue of our being Americans. Even when our charge was to study the international context in which we were placed in order to effectively translate the concept and constructs of difference into our classrooms, far too many colleagues were blinded their own displays of arrogance and as a result lost the opportunity to fully experience the richness of our environments.

Factoring in a New Dimension—Geopolitics

There are significant conceptual and practical drawbacks to changing strategies that view national culture as a distinct, overarching system for guiding actors' behaviors. This simple and deterministic view fails to factor in that it is possible for individuals or groups to be members of different cultures while at the same time residing within one major cultural context. While not close to the situation, I believe when we examine the current events that occurred in Turkey, Brazil, and Egypt as I was finishing this book, we will find credence to the plausibility of these propositions.

Each country in and of itself is a mecca for multiple cultural, economic, and religious contexts, which have many implications on government, economics, and the geopolitical strategies of the countries. Yet, when we read about the events in the news, there are few if any subtle or open references to the interplay of these dynamics—issues that can and will influence our ability to effectively work in environments that have strong geopolitical implications.

Geopolitics is a study of the influence of such factors as geography, economics, and demography on the politics and especially the foreign policy of a state.[1] The study of geopolitics also includes the study of the ensemble of relations between the interests of international political actors, interests focused to an area, space, geographical element or ways, and relations that create a geopolitical system.[2] Multidisciplinary in scope, geopolitics includes all aspects of the social sciences—with particular emphasis on political geography, international relations, the territorial aspects of political science, and international law.[3]

I am not an expert in geopolitics—in fact I have just begun to study the topic. However, during my visits to Turkey, I saw diversity aspects that could impact the success of geopolitical endeavors. However, as I began perusing the geopolitics literature, I have yet to see any substantive research regarding the diversity and intercultural considerations. I am still keeping hope alive that there is a body of research dedicated or at least beginning to be dedicated to understanding these diversity dynamics.

While I have not yet run across this body of research I hope exist or is at least emerging, it is not atypical, when reviewing the literature, to read many variations on the proposition that countries and organizations do not gravitate toward a universal model of economic success and organizational form as they attempt to cope with globalization. Rather, the mutual awareness that globalization entails invites them to use their unique economic, political, and social advantages as leverages in the global marketplace. Consequently, it is prudent to understand that their "uniqueness" in many instances can have multiple internal variations due to the diversity within their cultural domains.

So, while there appears to be a universal acknowledgment that these differences exist, their respective relationship to a concept—geopolitics—that is going to have significant impact upon our global strategies appears to be at this juncture warranting study and integration into the overarching concept and constructs associated with how countries geopolitically interact and leverage their relationships.

For example, let us examine Turkey, one of the actors in this recent play of global protesting. Turkey is a Eurasian country situated in the Anatolian peninsula located in Western Asia, and Eastern Thrace located in southeastern Europe. It is bordered by eight countries: Bulgaria to the northwest; Greece to the west; Georgia to the northeast; Armenia, Azerbaijan, and Iran to the east; and Iraq and Syria to the southeast. [4] The Mediterranean Sea and Cyprus are to the south; the Aegean Sea to the west; and the Black Sea is to the north. The Sea of Marmara, the Bosporus, and the Dardanelles (which together form the Turkish Straits) separate Europe and Asia.[5] So, what do you think are the cultural implications of its geography?

The demographics of Turkey have enhanced its ability to build effective alliances with Middle Eastern countries as well as with Europe. As a result, the economic downturn it experienced, which led to a stringent recovery program in 2002, quickly turned around, and now Turkey is a major economical player in multiple economic markets as well as geographic areas.[6]

When one views their businesses and their respective profiles, particularly the leadership profiles, across multiple sectors from a non-biased perspective, one will find that their ability to affect their significant market strength is tied to multiple variables, which include their religious and cultural orientation. Therefore, when we use Turkey as an example—and mind you there are many more countries with similar profiles—a researcher would have to use multiple lenses that would entail not only understanding the economic, social, and political realms of this country but concomitantly understanding how their culture, religion, and varying microcultural context informs their geopolitics.

There are those that suggest that in many country domains, cultural diversity has become a new goal of public policy. However, the uncertainty that surrounds its definition springs from the struggle for power (between different actors as well as between territorial levels) (Bonet and Negrier, 2011). Culture does have something to offer to policies of vertical integration. Yet, as countries expand their geopolitical strategies and corporations increasingly rely on the role of cities and regions in elaborating their global discourse and expanding, the possibility of a new intercultural destiny may emerge (2011). As a result, these possibilities call for movement beyond our propensity to assign causal links between cultural values and behaviors—actions that are far too reductionist and deterministic (Friedman and Antal, 2005).

For example, utilizing my example of and comments on the Guadeloupian culture, if I had entered that country expecting a static cultural context, be it French or a simplistic version of West Indian, I would have done significant disservice to my students, clients, colleagues, and friends who live in that country! Equally important, the geopolitics of Guadeloupe is as complex as is their culture. Situated in the French West Indies, the country is impacted and influenced by trade and the overarching political climate of the Caribbean. Yet, it is a department of France, which in and of itself places a different context on how the country will operate in the areas of government, trade, politics, and international relations.

Unfortunately, the typical strategy for understanding difference from an intercultural context is to delimit the valences of diversities and the even more refined microcultures that exist and neatly package people and their respective perceptions, proclivities, attitudes, and resulting behaviors into isolated paradigms and forget that they are continually informed by the actors involved in the "play" at that time. Equally important, the play and its resulting scenes are constantly morphing due to the changing dynamics of our global environment.

While I value the work of Geert Hofstede, Franz Trompenaars, Edgar Schein, and others who were responsible for the groundwork that began the intercultural dialogues, I also value the thoughts grounded in social construction theory, discourse analysis, and other methodologies and theoretical constructs that privilege the individual with the understanding that people come to the table every day socially constructing their environments—points that I believe Anzaldúa was making in her examination of the mestiza culture, albeit not using the "language" of postmodern organizational behavior. As geopolitics continues to morph, so will the resulting discourses around the concepts of difference. These conversations will have to emerge; you cannot get around the impact of difference on the constructs that make up the strategies associated with geopolitics.

While these perspectives, which move understanding and change strategies beyond the realm of "easy to do," may dismay organizational, political, and governmental leaders, they also should be perceived to be as hopeful even if cumbersome. You see, we have been working through "issues" associated with affecting organizational environments that value difference for far too long—irrespective of those differences residing in the landscape of one's home country or within an intercultural context.

If we are to effectively move forward and productively engage in a global environment that is ensconced with varieties of more hues than we can even begin to imagine, we have to be ready to enhance our understanding by utilizing more *complex* strategies for evoking a change and move beyond the vantage point of simple adaptation. Yes, the complexity of these strategies will make navigating them time consuming, and yes, they could be expensive. However, I suggest to any leader who is ready to embark upon this level of change that the sustaining outcomes will far outweigh the efforts and associated costs.

Years ago, when I was doing my undergraduate work, I remember tackling the issues of accommodation versus assimilation as I read and analyzed the work of noted psychologists Drs. Price Cobbs and William Grier. While in the 1970s one could find the suggestion of assimilation into a more mainstream culture a prevailing proposition, fast forwarding to the twenty-first century finds this proposition outdated.

The success of a manager in international business is not limited to, nor are they assessed by their ability to greet and eat politely according to the norms of a different culture (Neuert, Opel, and Schaupp, 2002). Yes, these abilities are important but the success of the manager is judged by the outcomes of interactions, in the form of the quality of ideas, decisions, or measures implemented, which means they need the ability to engage with people from many different backgrounds and cultures in order to achieve an understanding of each other's perception of reality when looking to work together (Neuert, Opel, and Schaupp, 2002).

Leaders and managers should understand the more salient dynamics and interplays between cultural context and behavioral constructs such as power, decision making, problem solving, and the actors' perceived position within and between these behavioral constructs. Inclusively augmenting this complex yet very personal and dynamic environment and interplay are the interactions between microcultures and the organizational context. And yes, racism, sexism, and all the other "isms" that we neatly package under the domain of "valuing diversity" are also underlays for many of the behavioral dynamics that will influence intercultural interactions—whether abroad or at home.

For example, in 2012, I suggested that when working in the African American community, researchers cannot allow themselves to fall victim to negating the uniqueness of their characteristics that do not always conform to Eurocentric models of change and research (Robinson-Easley, 2012). Their history, joys, and pain run deep, and should be acknowledged when they look to either embrace or help evoke change. These components help comprise who they are and in many respects constitute the foundation for their moving forward (Robinson-Easley, 2012). Therefore, researchers and intervention professionals need to be flexible when approaching the African American community in order to insure that they speak their truth; for it is only through understanding how they have internalized the realities of their truth can they begin to let go and change.

Concurring research suggest that qualitatively different approaches other than adaption should be used, which allows the opportunity to treat each interaction as unique and lays the foundational strategy for solving problems through observation, listening, experimentation, risk taking, and active involvement with others (Ratiu, 1983, as cited in Neuert, Opel, and Schaupp, 2002). These are critical concepts when we expand our work into other country domains. These are critical concepts when we hope to engage others in collaboration—true collaborations that are built upon foundations of trust and can withstand the tests of time.

I believe if Dr. Alvarez and I had formed our collegial partnership on a typical US model of exchange and research, we would not have had the success we did with our work, nor would we be, 11 years later, still collaborating. I chose to work within the European construct of getting to know your colleagues—a valuable lesson that I have continued to embrace throughout the years. As a result, the professional relationships I have developed throughout the years since she and I first met and I was introduced to that model have truly sustained the passage of time.

We can never walk away from the reality of the individual's experience, which should be the point of departure of any phenomenological analysis (Cone, 1970); this means that it does not matter that others will not share the reality of the actors involved in the change process. The change agents and/or managers or leaders involved in the interactions simply have to understand that the actor's reality, formed by multiple influences as described above is in fact their reality and is predicated upon their perceptions that frame their ontological perspectives of self (Robinson-Easley, 2012). I believe there is truth in the proposition that "we should engage with and use theories of action which can cope with change, power, variety, multiple influences—including the non-national—and the complexity and situational variability of the individual subject" (McSweeney, 2002, p. 113, as cited in Neuert, Opel, and Schaupp, 2002).

When working to develop diversity strategies or intercultural training, no amount of structural change processes can penetrate this reality. Organizational leaders might be able to obtain temporary compliance, but, at some point in time, the actors in the organizational story line will return to their "points of origin." Yet, the uniqueness of our journey and lessons learned, if critically deconstructed and analyzed, can become powerful tools for an organization looking to morph to the next level.

Deconstructing, thematically analyzing and sharing information relative to our discourse is indeed the *core* of the change process. Through disclosed patterns of discourse, we can understand the relational bonds that exist between people, and how structure is created, transformed, and maintained. And, through the study of discourse as a change process, we reinforce or, more importantly, challenge our beliefs (Barrett, Thomas, and Hocevar, 1995).

Neuert, Opel, and Schaupp, (2002) introduce the concept of negotiating reality, which involves surfacing the tacit knowledge and assumptions of parties involved in an interaction and bringing this knowledge to bear in the service of addressing a particular issue or problematic situation. While this engagement will not negate the overarching contours of culture, it allows the actors the opportunity to explore what lies under the surface of the cultural context—which shapes their perceptions, expectations, and behaviors as complex cultural beings (2002).

What intrigues me about this strategy are the three underlying concepts, which include (1) all people are of equal importance and worthy of equal respect, a point that completely should nullify the need for organizations to even remotely engage in "equal employment opportunity conversations," (2) as cultural beings, people differ because they possess different repertoires of ways of seeing and doing things, which drives the need to better understand microcultures, and, (3) the repertoire of no individual or group merits a priori superiority or right to dominance—a point that significantly embraces the need to embrace humanity rather than engaging in managing differences (Neuert, Opel, and Schaupp, 2002).

Furthermore, effectively negotiating reality avoids ethnocentrism and the paralysis inherent in simply accepting cultural differences. It does not ask people to shed their cultural repertoire and adapt to another culture, but rather to explore and test underlying assumptions as a basis for learning new ways of seeing and doing things effectively with other people from different backgrounds. Because the primary aim of negotiating reality is learning in a specific context, it differs from integration, which focuses on reconciling cultural differences and forging a multicultural identity (Neuert, Opel, and Schaupp, 2002). In other words, the concept and constructs of negotiating reality as suggested by the researchers, respects the individuality and humanity of the respective interacting actors.

Chapter Six

Contemporary Diversity Perspectives: More Lessons from the "Field"

New Orleans in 2005

While I clearly understood the microcultural differences that Dr. Alvarez and I addressed in our work, my subsequent research and field work took that learning to a vastly different level within my own cultural context, which did not include country cultural differences.

In 2004, a large, US-based African American Catholic organization examined and decided to use AI as its preferred change strategy throughout a sample of African American parishes and organizations in the United States (Easley, 2010). My role was to train pastors and lay leaders on AI and leadership development and spearhead the two critical projects, the Parish Pilot Programs and the Leadership Commissions, which were the two major components of this change initiative (Easley, 2010).

There were many issues facing each of the communities in which these parishes resided, such as blighted housing; high unemployment; subpar school districts; high incidents of crime, drugs, and disintegration of the family; and other varying problems that are typically found in socioeconomically challenged communities (2010). Although four parishes were selected for the pilot, the parish in New Orleans, Louisiana, was the largest and most aggressive parish in the project.

The processes for developing the change initiatives were grounded in AI and strategy implementation processes (2010). When I entered the engagement, I assumed that as an African American, I would better understand the culture and racial issues that African Americans in New Orleans faced. I was very wrong in that assumption (2010).

People live within interpretative communities, or discourse communities that provide a horizon of understanding that often serves as fact (Fish, 1999; Barrett et al., 1995, as cited in Easley, 2010). What I found was that many African Americans in New Orleans were historically rooted in class and caste systems and many identified themselves as Creole. Similar to the influence of Creole culture in the French Caribbean, the Creole culture had significant roots in the African American communities within New Orleans.

Although historically in New Orleans, Creoles made up the majority of the white population, emancipated slaves and their descendants tended to make up the middle class of the Creole society, with slaves who were household property representing the lowest class of Creoles. Within the Creole culture, there exists a complex social organization that emanated from this historical context, which also includes foreign groups, such as Germans, Irish, and Spaniards, whose names were given a French accent. All Creoles, no matter what level of society they were in, including slaves, looked down on the "Americans" (Bauman, 1992, as cited in Easley, 2010).

So, what did I learn from this experience? AI has resoundingly worked in communities and organizational contexts across the world. There is no question in my mind, having worked with it in prior professional endeavors, that the theoretical premises that are foundational to AI are sound. Yet, even though I was an African American woman working in an African American context, the events that occurred and impacted the initial results highly suggested that the lens through which I viewed the actors were significantly different than their personal lens (for more detail, please reference the article in the *Journal of Applied Behavioral Science*) (Easley, 2010).

Their microcultures, grounded in their Creole and Southern background, had to be privileged in order for them to move past the self-imposed boundaries. Yet, for that to happen, I had to acknowledge those boundaries. My limiting lens—I was working from the broader contexts of race and ethnicity.

Their linguistic representations and resulting behaviors, which seemed to be affected by the historical context of New Orleans, appeared to negatively affect their ability to move to a vision that embodied a full entitlement of rights, which were flourishing in other communities in New Orleans. As a result, when asked to engage in a vision of change, they were not strategically focused toward significant change. Their vision incorporated programmatic initiatives that would make little impact on a broad community basis. They appeared to hold on to linguistic patterns that were embedded in historical patterns of hopelessness and disconnection (Easley, 2010).

Any intervention strategy used in complex and diverse environments should begin to engage in a deeper level of sensemaking that goes beyond the surface to fully understand the many different layers of an individual. Equally important, whether you are in a community or traditional organization, it is prudent to question how we can really help actors authentically question how deep those layers of pain lie within their hearts and souls (Easley, 2010).

Intervention strategists need to learn about and critically deconstruct the *historical* context that is limiting the formation of new linguistic forms and paradigms—which, if not done effectively, will significantly delimit total engagement within the organizational context. In other words, we learn that a critical component of our change initiatives involve negotiating all realms of the realities of the actors involved within the change process. A failure to do so will once again only produce limiting, if at all desired, change.

What was equally important for me to learn in this process was, as noted by Neuert, et al. (2002), that as cultural beings, people really do differ because they possess different repertoires of ways of seeing and doing things, and the repertoire of no individual or group merits a priori superiority or right to dominate. I quickly learned that I was limited by the fact that I had never lived in the South; did not understand Southern culture, particularly African American Southern culture; and was completely unfamiliar with the Creole culture (Easley, 2010). My major lesson—there should have been more theoretical sensitivity on my part, toward understanding the possible depth as well as range of the actors' perceptions and plausible interpretive schemas before I entered the organization (Easley, 2010).

Organizational leaders make the same mistakes. They tend to take for granted that because people are a part of their organization, they will automatically embrace the vision of the organization and adhere to the values of the leadership.

Nichols (1994) provided an important perspective when she recanted the experiences of one very successful entrepreneur.

This entrepreneur decided to expand his thinking and enter seminary (needless to say, I clearly resonate with what can drive an individual to that decision). The owner was looking for ways to change both his company and himself. Exploring philosophers and theologians, he came to believe that common values along with a shared sense of purpose can turn a company into a community—thereby invoking a deeper meaning with respect to work and more personal satisfaction (Nichols, 1994).

Interestingly, Nichols critiqued this perspective by suggesting that these relationships, which are still ensconced in inequality in power and incentives, really does not "pass the test with workers." Despite the owner engaging in the development of a new mission statement with input from his workforce, he still found fear and distrust running rampant throughout the organization and across the ranks of both management and labor (Nichols, 1994).

I sincerely believe that the heart of this entrepreneur was in the right place and that he was truly seeking answers to looming questions. There are many well-meaning organizational leaders who are looking to evoke positive change within the organizations. Unfortunately, within our traditional MBA and other business schools, we tend not to effectively link the concepts of organizational effectiveness with valuing the human spirit and embracing humanity in order to really bring out the best in people. So, while this organizational leader attempted to move to a more transcendent focus on his people, he still encountered barriers.

Our propensity is to broadly characterize people (as I did), especially when our personal comfort zones cause us to suggest similarities that may or may not exit, thereby failing to account for the individual differences that can and will impact how they engage in sensemaking.

A few days after I had my last session in New Orleans, Hurricane Katrina hit the city. I was truly blessed by the fact that I left the city three days before evacuation began. But my heart was torn as I watched the evacuation processes from afar.

There were numerous paradoxes that are similar in context to the propositions Nichols raised (1994). Leaders of that city had purported change. Yet, I likened the stories (actually in a paper I wrote for one of my seminary classes) of survivors who evacuated New Orleans to the conditions of the Middle Passage and mindset of slave captors. Some of you might see this analogy as a stretch, but flow with me and insert yourself into the lens of people who lived in that city—similar to what organizational leaders should do when purporting change in their respective organizations. You see, the "progress" a leader purports might be viewed by the lens of the actors as something very different.

Deplorable conditions were the norm during the Middle Passage; and they were the same during the Katrina evacuation processes. African Americans were forced to lie next to people who for days were dying in their own waste. As one woman recounted:

> The worse experience for me was being alone for maybe four days in the airport. That's something I will never forget. There were bodies. There were people bleeding. There were people lying in their own waste. One after another. If you take Gone with the Wind and the Nazi War and the Vietnam war, and visualize that in one place, that's how I would describe the airport. When you watch it on TV, it's like watching a Walt Disney versus an R-rated movie. You can only see what they want you to see. You can't smell it. (Perry, 2005, p. 1)

Similar to the process for kidnapping Africans and transporting them to America, families in New Orleans were separated for extended periods of time, and traumatized by the failure to communicate with one another in concert with their inability to obtain information from relief agencies. Initially, the only way people who possessed cell phones could contact one another was by text messaging (Augustine, 2006). However, what appeared to be the most traumatizing was the movement from the Superdome to the Astrodome in Houston. Families were separated on buses, and were told that the buses were going to the same locations, only to find little children several states removed from their parents (Augustine, 2006). And, if they weren't removed to other states, some were found dead.

> When we woke up Friday morning, we heard that a couple of kids were missing. Later on, they were found in the bathroom with their throats slit and possibly raped. I'm talking young kids—from the ages six to eight. I didn't see anything, but the parents verified that their children were found dead. Word gets around in an enclosed place like that. (Perry, 2005, p. 4)

In addition to these atrocities were countless stories of police brutality, instances where the Red Cross workers displayed public disdain for the African American citizens of this city and worse, African Americans turning on each other. When housed in the Superdome and Astrodome, people were afraid to sleep or go to the bathroom. It was not uncommon to hear stories of rape and theft. When going to use the public facilities, people were compelled to travel in groups for safety (Augustine, 2006).

While these actions are extreme—we still hear of atrocities that people of color, women, individuals with different sexual orientation, or individuals with disabilities incur within varying organizational contexts. When I visited New Orleans in 2010, I saw no reason for African Americans to believe that the rebuilding of New Orleans was going to include them—and/or invoke a more egalitarian environment/city.

A couple of years ago, I saw a documentary that addressed these issues, yet when I questioned the film makers as to what recommendations should have been made at the end of the documentary, they looked at me as if I were speaking a foreign language. Once again, I had to question—why raise the issue if you are not going to go deep enough to provoke a conversation regarding "real" change?

As Africans were removed from their country and homes for reasons ensconced in both racism *and* economics during the Middle Passages, history repeated itself. There are considerable undertones as well as overt accusations that post-Katrina strategies are racially and economically focused, but to the detriment of New Orleans's poor. The city was very slow in relocating people back to New Orleans. Similar to the diaspora Africans endured during the slave trade, post-Katrina African Americans were still being subjugated to living in a diaspora.

Fast forward this example to an organizational context—you develop your diversity and/or intercultural management programs, yet glass ceilings still occur even in today's environment. People from different racial, gender and/or cultural contexts face limited opportunities to rise to the top ranks, salary discrepancies continue to prevail between men and women with the same and/or similar educational and experiential backgrounds, yet organizations want to purport that they have moved beyond the need for affirmative action and are embracing diversity and cross culturalism in a global context!

So, whether we are looking at the Middle Passages, the aftermath of Hurricane Katrina, or a contemporary strategy to evoke equality into a workplace—it is still difficult to delimit the injustices that permeate these change initiatives because the humanity of the individual is still not fully embraced.

Adding insult to injury, companies worldwide through the United Nation's Global Leadership Compact, which began a few years ago (to be discussed in a later chapter) are still addressing these issues in global organizations.

I know I am repeating myself when I say this, but if we are to truly embrace difference we cannot allow ourselves to be "selective." Over the course of many classes, graduate and undergraduate management courses, I have students extensively explore ethical and social responsibility violations in an effort to deconstruct their origins and opportunities for remediation within the domains of leadership development, organizational behavior, and organization development via recommended strategies.

In each class, as students present their findings, the class just sits there and shakes their heads; some, including myself, break down and cry. The travesties and failure to respect people defy logic. Yet, we continue to manage diversity from the same lens we looked through years ago. We fail to understand that respecting and loving people are not just characteristics that can selectively be developed. They have to permeate every aspect of our interactions.

CHAPTER SEVEN

THE MOVEMENT TOWARD NEW DIVERSITY QUESTIONS AND PARADIGMS: SYNTHESIZING MY LEARNING

As a researcher and a change agent, I am constantly analyzing my experiences and the resulting knowledge. When I first began working with diversity change strategies, my work largely focused on strategically and systemically addressing the whole organization. Having worked in organizations that did not drive their diversity initiatives from the top levels, I clearly understood how critical it was for senior leaders to articulate a diversity vision that would fully represent their support.

I had grown tired of working with diversity councils, training initiatives, and other forms of band-aid approaches that largely represented grass roots efforts, or support from mid-level managers who had little power, but were deeply committed to driving diversity change within the organization. The simple fact was, if the leadership of the organization was not prepared to take a stand on diversity, anything else would fall short.

I also understood how organizational cultures could stymie change. Over the course of my career, I had worked with enough passive aggressive or passive defensive cultures to understand that when people want to end-run change, they are well-equipped to do so. Consequently, I deeply felt, and still do, that it is very important for organizational change agents to understand organizational culture.

However, in the next phase of my learning I began to deconstruct what really constituted organizational culture and its interface with diversity. Subjective feelings of the actors in an organization can and do impact all aspects of the organization's work, which is why I believe that the research Dr. Alvarez conducted is such an important contribution to the literature. I am sure the organizational leaders who were structuring the merger and acquisition of those three hospitals never even thought to engage in an analysis of the actor's respective microcultures. After all, they were all French citizens and worked in a French hospital—a similar perspective to the case of the hospital president I previously referenced. Remember, he believed that because he had mostly people of color (despite their originating from different country, culture, and microcultural contexts) working in the nursing and physician positions, the hospital did not have a diversity problem!

As previously stated, for the past three years I have taught intercultural management to MBA students in the French West Indies. The individuals with whom I work are French citizens and lived in France before coming to Guadeloupe to develop the educational facility that is linked to one of the French universities. One evening last year while having dinner at the home of the director, one of the individuals—a female—was sharing pictures of her family who lives in another French West Indies island. I was amazed when I looked at her pictures. While I have learned so much teaching intercultural management in this social and economic context and had opportunities to examine the interplay between culture, identity, and other microcultural issues, I was not prepared to see the amazing hue of color in her family. Although I have worked with and known her for three years, I had "categorized" her as being "white" (which is a typical distinction between those that live in the French West Indies versus those that come from France, where she previously lived). Never in a million years would I have imagined her to have so much "color" in her bloodline and culture. The interesting fact that I am constantly reminded of as I travel is that we can never "assume." The fact that she comes from a very multiracial background informs her identity in ways I would have never assumed.

I have learned to be clear on the issues of identity, race, nationalism, and culture that distinguish those who live in the French Caribbean from those in France, even those considered "white" in the French West Indies. However, what I learned was that those differences may be far more subtle than we can readily identify—a point that was reinforced with my work in New Orleans.

The work in New Orleans set the stage for my 2010 publication in the *Journal of Applied Behavioral Sciences* (Easley, 2010). My experiences reinforced the need for my internalizing a point of reference and strategy that would move the researcher and the respective actors toward a more in-depth understanding and conversation regarding the varying dimensions of culture that reside within the respective community and/or organization.

Sharing race is simply not enough common ground for people to really engage with and understand one another. While I understood microcultural differences between Dr. Alvarez and me, my experiences in New Orleans took the understanding of microcultural differences to a new level. Even nuances such as socioeconomic differences can cause a significant bridge between people who come from the same racial background.

So, when working in organizations, how should we prepare ourselves to be effective when we begin to work toward change? As I learned my lessons through the school of "hard knocks," I also learned that it is vitally important for a researcher or change agent to take "doing their homework" to a new level. Therefore, in the model I designed that was featured in the *Journal of Applied Behavior Sciences* (since modeling is how I focus on my sensemaking), the initial steps suggested that the change agent engage in *extensive* research with respect to the cultural dynamics of the community or organization with whom he or she is working (2010).

Similar to the concept of ethnographic research, those initial steps proposed that acquiring knowledge about a particular context could provide insight into nondiscursive material or cultural understandings of the actors. Yet, I also understood and still concur that there is also a negative that can emerge from this type of advanced research. The preparation, if not careful, can also impose a bias that can negatively impact the intervention for change. Consequently, I suggested that the change agent would have to be very sensitive and focused on avoiding preconceived biases. Yet, the downside of not doing this type of "pre-work" is having information on only the emerging discourse of the actors during the change strategy, which may be insufficient given that many conversations and resulting insight remain at the tacit level (Polanyi, 1967) typically predicated upon unspoken assumptions that actively guide behavior. (Hansen, 2006; Easley, 2010).

Even if we closely examine war and conflicts that are prevalent in the twenty-first century, particularly those that reside within one country context, one should ask—when you move aside the economic and political issues, how much of that conflict results from the microcultural differences that can and do pull people apart? Albeit new to the study of the topic, as I have begun to study geopolitics I wonder how much in-depth attention should be given from the social science perspective to the microcultural variances that will occur as countries collaborate. Should the current thinking on spatial politics incorporate much more investigation on the variances of human behavior and diversities when examining the political climate?

When I wrote my 2010 article, I concluded then, as I do now, that many culturally diverse organizations and communities in today's world face a multiplicity of challenges that are augmented by many layers of culture. Yet people want change and today's organizational leaders cannot afford to not invoke change. Our global economic, political, spatial world is dramatically changing. Alliances are being formed all over the world that call for a deeper level of understanding of the actors that will collaboratively work. We have no choice as we move through this millennium but to challenge our praxes. For example, as the editorial team and I have moved through various stages of this book, the United States and other global nations took a stance against Syria. In a number of classes, my students made their political commentaries on what they thought the position of the United States and the US allies should be. Yet, I had to bring to their attention the possibility that while the issues of humanity were at the top of the agenda due to the overarching allegations, there were political challenges that were concomitantly based upon cultural alliances as well as political and economic alliances/challenges that took this problem to a very different level of complexity. Culture always has to be factored in, especially when you are looking at the dynamics of a region, and in some cultural/country contexts religious commonalities will also play a role.

I clearly understand that this information can be overwhelming. Equally important, I also understand that organizational leaders, when factoring in all that they do, may simply say that they do not have time to delve this deep into people. And just as many may feel that it is unwarranted. But there is a reality we cannot get away from. People are complex. The results of the work I have done over the years have raised many questions and challenges to many of the traditional paradigms I learned regarding identity, sensemaking, and change, particularly as they pertain to communities and/or organizations that span ethnicities and cultures (2010). Gaining a better understanding of these issues is what led me to seminary. I had to learn how to better understand the hearts and souls of people because it was becoming very clear to me that the learning I obtained in studying organization development and organizational behavior was insufficient when compared and contrasted to the complexities of today's global society.

Yet, I also know that when we work to evoke change in organizations and/or communities that are culturally diverse, we have to consider challenging our own guiding praxes and work toward understanding their very specific and fragile patterns of life. In 2010 when I wrote that article, as I do now, I respectfully suggest that to be successful in our diversity strategies as well as in our intercultural work, we have to challenge what we "know" before we look to facilitate change (2010).

At this stage, you as the reader may be wondering, how do I work through all of this if I am truly working toward building an organization that values difference? As a professional in organization development, I will not close this book without providing a proposed roadmap.

As I have researched, consulted to, and worked in organizations where I relied upon contemporary strategies, theories, and resounding propositions, I also found that they did not always work, as evidenced by the many pages relegated to my personal experiences, in contexts that are diverse and populated by people who have faced many levels of *strife* over their lives.

My learning is very simple—strategies replete with Eurocentric psychologies that tend to be framed with a significant amount of bias and/or failure to acknowledge the many hues of difference generally will not be designed to delve deep into the organization's cultural and subcultural contexts (including the many microcultures that will reside within those contexts).

One can even question as to whether or not those that research and write in these areas are doing so in a bias-free environment. Colleges and universities within the United States have for years been under attack for its lack of representation of difference.

As previously referenced, in 2011 colleagues and I contributed to a book that addressed the many issues facing faculty of color in the landscape of higher education—where our research and academic perspectives on topics such as diversity emanate.

When researching my contributing chapter, I found the academic literature to be full of peer-reviewed journal articles that addressed recruitment and retention issues associated with minority faculty, disparities in promotion and tenure, and the lack of sustaining faculty development programs. More salient issues included minority faculty being penalized when they researched and published on issues related to race and ethnicity, largely because top tier journals are reluctant to publish this work (Easley, 2011). They are counter to master narratives, and troubling to master narratives in the editorial-review processes; they draw implications and make recommendations for researchers invested in nonmainstream educational research in higher education (Stanley, 2007, as cited in Easley, 2011). Yet, who is to say that the master narratives have the most accurate perspective? Equally important, who is to say that they are the prevailing narratives in today's diverse global environment? As I have written this book, my literature review has spanned multiple country contexts and researchers. My conclusion—I challenge the concept and constructs associated with what was identified as a "master" narrative. The kaleidoscope of diversity has truly changed that paradigm!

In 2004, the lack of diverse faculty in educational administrative programs was cited as a challenge to the preparation of educational leaders and administrators, and in 2006 it was noted that although the demographic landscape in the United States has dramatically changed in the last ten years with African Americans, Hispanics, and American Indians /Alaska Natives together comprising over 25 percent of the total US population, the racial makeup of the nation's medical school faculty presents a starkly different picture, with a continued underrepresentation in medicine (Bramble, 2006, as cited in Easley, 2011).

An equally disturbing salient point of continued oppression and discriminatory practices in the hiring of African Americans into higher education was the privileging of white women over African American candidates (Hall, 2006, as cited in Easley, 2011). More specifically, in 2005, an investigation of white women and people of color (primarily African Americans) employed as faculty at Ivy League institutions was conducted and reported to the public. Statistical data confirmed a much greater ability on the part of white women to gain employment at such prestigious institutions. Institutions similar in prestige to the Ivy League suggested the existence of similar patterns—a continued pattern of white domination, albeit a shift in gender (Hall, 2006, as cited in Easley, 2011).

An internal issue relative to retention, often overlooked or ignored is that of a "chilly climate," which in one study was defined as a climate of respect and support, often recognized by the social distance between majority and minority group faculty and administrators and by the equitability of work assignments (Turner, Myers Jr., and Creswell, 1999, as cited in Easley, 2011). Although many Black faculty members are forewarned about the environment and its issues within predominately white institutions, its reality becomes much clearer as they engage in research, teaching, and service (Cole, 2001, as cited in Easley, 2011).

So you see, even the environment from which research on critical topics of difference emerge is not beyond their challenges when it comes to valuing difference. Consequently, when looking to evoke change in an organization, one needs to be very careful when embracing the "current" thinking on a topic that is of such importance to our world.

Part II

Nontraditional Venues for Evoking the Diversity Conversation

CHAPTER EIGHT
MOVING THE CONVERSATION BEYOND THE ETHICS LITERATURE: CONNECTING DIVERSITY AND SOCIAL RESPONSIBILITY

Over the years that I have taught ethics and social responsibility, I have been amazed at how many organizations researched by my students were either directly involved in or had a significant role in sustaining work conditions in major cities *and* developing countries that defied logic. The list of offenders is long, and over the years the level of negative impact has not lessened. However, the challenges of globalization have made it necessary to conduct a thorough investigation into the conditions of human life as they stand today (Wulf, 2013). There is a globalization of poverty, suffering, war, terror, and the exploitation and destruction of nature; conditions that appear to be related to colonialism and capitalism and unfortunately are being ignored when it comes to evoking systemic change (2013).

However, the purpose of this chapter is not to single out specific industries, global economies where these issues reside, or cite specific corporate examples. Most of us know who the players are—current players as well as the historical ones who have the distinction of being specifically cited in the ethics literature for bad practices.

The purpose of this chapter is to posit questions regarding the intersection of these issues to the failure to value our humanity and ask a hard question—is this failure to value our humanity tied to our failure to evoke an equalitarian environment where these travesties would never reside? In other words, is there a real separation between the diversity, social responsibility, and the ethics literatures? Are the underlying premises that drive people to make the decisions as to how they will operate similar? Are the attitudes regarding difference similar?

I am sure we can make countless pro and con points looking across multiple literature streams—starting with the literature on attitudes and beliefs. However, once again, my point is not to argue the merits of those literature streams. My point is simply to be provocative and point out the disconnects I have personally dealt with over the years as both an actor in many of these venues, and as a teacher who has to construct connections for students to critically examine, research, and come back with their own propositions. Each time I have asked students to examine the issues, they tend to draw the same conclusions for a beginning discussion as I have. In other words, they too find more commonalities than differences regarding the etiology of behaviors on the part of organizations that domestically as well as internationally seem to have "issues" with difference.

My first eye-opening experience with the varying issues of social responsibility, its intersection with diversity and dichotomous practices that can and do emerge when people of color are factored into the equation came during my employment with Union Carbide Corporation, where I worked during the Bhopal, India situation that is cited in numerous ethics books. My first "serious" academic awakening was in my first year as a doctoral student in organization development. One of the initial books we read was Dr. David Korten's book *When Corporations Rule the World*. The propositions in Korten's book were eye opening. He was and still is clearly ahead of his time.

Korten attributes the depletion of natural, human, social, and institutional capital almost exclusively to the "Midas curse" of a global financial capitalistic system (Gladwin, 1998). Yet, in concert with the global environmental and social declines, which can in part be contributed to finance capitalism, people also must factor in the social decapitalization factors (1998). These factors specifically incorporate human rights abuse, gender bias, and human health insecurity, which may be more directly related to factors such as patriarchy, ethnic strife, political fragmentation, rapid urban development, and other similar issues (1998).

I often ask several questions of my students when we examine business ethics and social responsibility. My first question for them is whether or not we should define socially responsible behaviors in the context of the social and cultural time periods in question. In other words, societal conditions 20 years ago may have little to no relevance in today's global economy. Consequently, when we examine the historical contexts, while that history is important to understand, we also have to understand the critical dimensions and nuances of the current state, which also suggests that we challenge the tried and true strategies used to invoke change.

The rapidity of today's global society in developing and more fully developed countries require those participating in economic and social development to be more systemically focused on the implications and plausible interpretations of their actions. For example, the rapid development of today's global economic systems and structures call for a more fully educated and technologically developed workforce. Yet, a few years ago, the International Labor Organization estimated that close to 250 million children between the ages of 5 and 14 work full time and grow up without schooling and other activities. A total of 60 percent of those working children live in Asia, mainly South Asia, with a further 32 percent located in Africa (McClintock, 2001).

And, while the majority of child labor occurs in less developed countries, small pockets of illegal child labor still are found in industrialized economies, largely in agriculture enterprises, services, and in small-scale manufacturing subcontracting to larger enterprises (2001). There are many complex factors that contribute to child labor. The economic instability of the country and family structure can significantly drive the need for every member of the family to work. Many developing countries have developing infrastructures—government, laws, educational systems, and so on, that make regulating these issues quite challenging and cumbersome. Consequently, while the "existence" of child labor may be unavoidable in many country contexts, the conditions to which children are exposed and the work hours can in fact be regulated by the employing organization, which raises the need to address the second question I typically ask my class. Similar points are associated with the argument for and against sweatshops—which are addressed later in this chapter.

My second question is whether or not moral notions like responsibility and obligation should be applied to groups such as corporations, or are the *individual people* in the organization the only real moral agents? Is the organization as a "whole" responsible for their actions and/or lack of action or is there a need for the organization to systemically deconstruct the role of transformative leadership in today's environment? I also address this point a little further into the chapter by beginning a dialogue regarding proposed constructs that may impact how leaders make decisions as to how the organization will treat individuals who reside in challenged environments.

Whether a corporate leader, head of an NGO, or of a government entity, can leaders afford not to look at the issues facing both their organizations and the social and economic contexts in which they live and work from a systems oriented lens? If leaders and their respective management teams are truly the moral agents of the organization, what do their actions say about these individuals when they fail to require their organizations and any tiered subcontractor to respect the humanity of those they employ? Is this any different from the diversity issues we face in our local environments?

The literature is full of arguments regarding legal compliance versus voluntary compliance when it comes to evoking fair labor practices, livable wages, and decent working conditions for individuals that reside in developing countries. Are these just lower-level dialogues of the aforementioned equal employment opportunity laws that we still have trouble complying with in many developed nations? Why does it feel that in 2013, there is still a need to say *"Now is the time to lift our national policy from the quicksand of racial injustice to the solid rock of human dignity"*? (Rev. Dr. Martin Luther King Jr., Letter from Birmingham Jail).[1]

If I cannot invoke an equalitarian environment within the domains of all the geographies in which I operate, how then can I, as an organizational leader, evoke the proposition that I value and manage diversity within my national domain? Albeit these being rhetorical questions, I believe they are questions that need to be more fully explored when we engage in a conversation regarding diversity, intercultural management, and valuing "difference."

My third critical question for my students is: How can we identify and better understand the *intersection* between leadership, culture, power, and ethical decision making in an organizational environment when we are looking at issues of social justice across multiple domains? And, please keep in mind that when I use the term organization, I am loosely addressing all organizational contexts, which will include communities, government, and other forms of structures that interact with the population at large and their socioeconomic contexts.

I ask these questions because the critical issues we have to grapple with relative to ethics and social responsibility in today's environment, in my opinion, surpass the questions we asked years ago. When we discuss social responsibility and its intersection with other organizational behaviors in concert with the concepts and constructs of diversity and intercultural management, we are typically working through issues that pertain to actions and decisions that consider the legal, economic, and societal factors in the short and long run as well as organizational interests. I totally agree that there are multiple variables that should be addressed. The economics of a developing country is going to call for a different level of analysis and decision making. Yet, I cannot quite understand how people can associate the outcomes of those decisions to decisions as to how fairly people should be treated when addressing working conditions, humane treatment, constructive hours, and fair wages.

While there are many organizations that lay claim to exemplary records of socially responsible actions, such as significant financial contributions to at-risk communities, educational sponsorships, financing infrastructure projects—and the list goes on, there are an equal number that are continuing to evoke very negative impacts upon our global society.

A beginning list of issues includes:

- Environmental pollution, which is still an ongoing issue despite our push toward a green environment. One only has to look at the major faux pas of the oil industry over the past few years, the demographic makeup of the most impacted communities and far too many lackluster attempts to remediate the long-term economic impact of spills and halfhearted cleanups;
- Poor quality and unsafe work environments;
- Violations to the equal employment opportunity laws;
- Health issues have been a consistent published concern by many watch groups due to multiple studies indicating direct correlation between the increased rate of infectious diseases and manufacturing pollutants.

Large corporations exist in many forms—multinationals, transnationals, and so on. However, those that have expanded internationally, and particularly within developing countries, tend to have two sides to their perceived impact (Westaway, 2012). While growth in power and influence within the context of globalization has been significant, there are many who argue that the impact of these entities, despite developing countries making great strides to attract them for their economic influence on jobs, housing, and country wealth, have also had their challenges. The power and influence of the internationally stratified corporation has the ability to adversely impact human rights, which calls for a different dialogue regarding human rights (2012). These organizations hold significant power and influence. Corporations that operate within a multinational arena have rewritten many of the rules of economic engagement and as a result have challenged the established principles of juridical boundaries and state sovereignty (Westaway, 2012). Jochnick (1999) argues that they exert an inordinate influence over local laws and policies and their impact on human rights range from a direct role in violations, such as abuse of employees or the environment, to indirect support of governments guilty of widespread repression (as cited in Westaway, 2012).

For example, many people still remember the Union Carbide chemical leak in Bhopal, India (Stephens, 2002); the Nike, Disney, and Levi Strauss sweatshops in countries such as Indonesia (Nazeer, 2011); the Wal-Mart factories in China and Honduras (Clade and Weston, 2006); the case of Royal Dutch/Shell in Ogoni, Nigeria (Wiwa, 2000); the operations of Unocal Oil Corporation in Myanmar (Chambers, n.d.), the policies of British Petroleum in Columbia (Human Rights Watch, 1998), the actions of Texaco in Ecuador, and the Freeport-McMoRan in Indonesia (Balland, 2001) (as cited in Westaway, 2012).

If we closely examine just these few that are on this list, we will also see subpar performance within their own national domains. The list of complaints and lawsuits against Wal-Mart, with respect to gender bias, and many other forms of discrimination is long, and who can forget the Texaco fiasco in the late 1990s that occurred shortly after the 1993 law suit filed on behalf of the people in Ecuador?[2] More specifically,

> Critics of affirmative action routinely argue that the effort is no longer necessary because discrimination is now dead. Nothing disproves that theory as emphatically as the emerging scandal at Texaco,

where senior executives have been caught on tape deriding minority employees in racist terms—and plotting to destroy documents subpoenaed in a Federal discrimination case.

The tapes are excerpted in papers filed in Federal District Court in White Plains, where Texaco is based. The excerpts, reported this week by Kurt Eichenwald of The Times, come from a meeting held in August 1994 during which three senior executives discussed a class-action lawsuit filed by black employees who charged that Texaco had discriminated against them and created a racially hostile atmosphere. The Federal Equal Employment Opportunity Commission essentially validated the suit, ruling that there was reason to believe Texaco guilty of company-wide racial bias.

Transcripts of the August tapes leave little doubt about the atmosphere at the company. Senior executives, including Texaco's former treasurer Robert Ulrich, freely deride black employees as "niggers" and "black jelly beans."[3]

The United Nations' Efforts

In 2004, the United Nations chaired by Secretary-General Kofi Annan, assembled hundreds of corporate executives, government officials, and civil society leaders at UN headquarters on June 24 to take stock of the Global Compact and chart its future course. President Luis Inácio Lula da Silva of Brazil delivered the keynote luncheon address.[4]

The ten principles adopted by the Global Compact included the following:

Human Rights
1. Businesses should support and respect the protection of internationally proclaimed human rights.
2. Make sure that businesses are not complicit in human right abuses.

Labour
3. Businesses should uphold the freedom of association and the effective recognition of the right to collective bargaining.
4. The elimination of all forms of forced and compulsory labor.
5. The effective abolition of child labor.
6. The elimination of discrimination in respect of employment and occupation.

Environment

7. Businesses should support a precautionary approach to environmental challenges.
8. Undertake initiatives to promote greater environmental responsibility.
9. Encourage the development and diffusion of environmentally friendly technologies.

Anti-corruption

10. Businesses should work against corruption in all its forms, including extortion and bribery.[5]

The United Nations also launched The Women's Empowerment Principles—Equity Means Business. The Women's Empowerment Principles are a set of principles for business offering guidance on how to empower women in the workplace, marketplace, and community. They evolved from collaborations between the UN Women and the UN Global Compact. The development of the principles included an international multi-stakeholder consultation process, which was launched in March 2009.[6] The principles are designed to emphasize the business case for corporate action to promote gender equality and women's empowerment. They are said to be informed by real-life business practices and inputs gathered from across the globe.[7]

Yet, if we revisit the propositions of the Hudson Institute in the late 1980s, women were cited to soon become a significant percent of the US workforce. However, as previously stated, women still make (in the same jobs) less than men and we are still "talking" about equality for women domestically and globally. What has really changed, locally and globally?

While many may want to engage other literatures to either counter or support my propositions, my purpose for bringing forth these questions is simple—if you do not value me locally and globally, is there really a separation between social responsibility and diversity/intercultural management challenges or again, as I will suggest, are we discussing two sides of the same and/or similar coin?

Quite frankly, I welcome a debate, because I sincerely believe it is time we stop separating the literatures (ethics, social responsibility, diversity, and intercultural management) and the resulting discourse and look at the etiology of the multiple, yet very complex issues from the domicile of our inability to value humanity—home and abroad! Perhaps if we engage in an authentic debate we can begin to evoke a more serious challenge to these issues. And, I hope and pray that in the midst of debate, thoughtful contemplation, or even the choice to meditate on the questions I pose, perhaps better ideas will morph into strategies that have the potential to change the world in which we live. However, we should be realistic—there are many people who are comfortable with the way in which we globally live now. Yet, as noted in the beginning of the book, there are many, many people who are beginning to feel their pain at such a level that they are refusing to stand still.

We have options. We have the ability to plant the seeds of true transformational change, instead of allowing our world to erupt into a crisis.

Dr. Robert Quinn, who I truly believe is one of the most inspiring and leading researchers in the discipline of leadership, provides a simple example on our ability to influence change. When we plant seeds, which I am hoping to do with this book, it is a process of creative tension. Yet, from the interactive process a new form may emerge. In one sense the outcome is determined, because if you plant an acorn, you will have oak tree and not a maple tree, but in another sense, the process is also free, emergent, or self-organizing. The number and placement of branches in that oak tree and other characteristics of the adult tree will depend on a variety of interactions with the environment (Quinn, 2000).

Changing human systems is similar, whether one person evokes the change or many. We are always interacting with our environments, which over time become patterned or normalized (Quinn, 2000). People develop scripts and collective cultures, with the scripts structuring the individual and the cultures structuring the collective. The scripts and cultures resemble the shell of the seed. If they crack, we can begin to interact with our environment in new ways, which can give rise to a new self and a new collective—inviting the opportunity to transform (Quinn, 2000).

So, again, I respectfully suggest that in the midst of reading what I have written, new seeds are being planted that have the potential to emerge into something far greater than what we currently experience.

Are Our Failures to Be Globally Socially Responsible and Our Lackluster Diversity Efforts Two Sides of the Same Coin?

First and foremost, I am the first to acknowledge that within cultures, there are perspectives toward gender and ethnicity that are indigenous to that culture that will never parallel my lens. I acknowledge that these differences exist, which is an important part of valuing difference. I also understand that in some countries, women will never be equal to men in the home or the boardroom. However, those are not the organizational environments and cultural contexts that I am addressing in this chapter.

I also understand that when examining the issues that reside in developing countries, one needs to factor in that the public administrative systems in many countries are still developing; as are their countries. And, I equally acknowledge that when we examine issues of child labor, we also have to be sensitive to issues that speak to how families make money in communities where poverty exists at levels to which many of us have not been exposed.

There are many differences that separate developing countries from those that are more fully developed. Yet, one must question why many of the businesses that come into these countries make the decision not to uplift the workforce. Are they faceless to business leaders or do organizations rationalize that they do not have to get too close to the situation to ponder whether or not the improvement of working conditions and treatment of employees are the correct actions? Or, do members of privileged groups tend to share a dominate worldview, which they define, thereby seeking no reason to question their perspectives and paradigms? Is it possible that along with a self-perceived sense of normalcy comes as sense of superiority? Equally thought provoking, if poverty and oppression are recognized, would those who are privileged be so comfortable because in the background looms the possibility of loss of their privilege (Goodman, 2001, as cited in Kravitz, 2002)?

Perhaps, to be able to deal competently with these issues that also reside within a domain of diversity, we need to experience the *Other*. Neither people nor cultures can develop if they cannot mirror themselves in others (Wulf, 2013). Yet, we also have to be real as to how we have engaged in a reductionist view of alterity (2013). Similar to Akbar's propositions, Wulf has suggested that the Western rationality of logocentrism has led to foreign cultures and people being judged according to their adherence to logocentric norms. Equally critical, Western individuality and the egocentrism that goes with it increases the ability of those in power to assert individualist needs at the cost of community, and lastly, the concept of overvaluation of ethnocentrism diminishes an appreciation of other cultures (Wulf, 2013). Yet, I am drawn to repeat Rev. Dr. Howard Thurman's poignant words on the interplay of change.

> Always there is some voice that rises up against what is destructive, calling attention to an alternative, another way. It is a matter of more than passing significance that the racial memory as embodied in the myths of creation, as well as in the dream of prophet and seer, points ever to the intent to community as the purpose of life. (Thurman, 1963, p. 94)

Answers to the issues require a different lens when deconstructing issues and engaging multiple organizational contexts, such as corporations, NGOs, and social service agencies in an effort to help evoke change. Neither people nor cultures can change and/or develop unless those who are in positions of power can experience the *Other* (Wulf, 2013).

Equally important, there should be broad agreement *and* commitment on what constitutes the public interest between business, unions, governments, and other interests, in concert with sufficient institutional continuity in the private and public sectors to maintain and develop a social contract that can bring forth change (McClintock, 2001).

Greater transparency in the process of public cooperation is necessary and concomitantly requires that the enterprise—business, union, government or nonprofit—should be sufficiently open and accessible to public view so that informed judgments may be made by both internal and external groups and stakeholders (McClintock, 2001). However, it is clear that all will not want to engage in that conversation.

When I teach international organizational behavior, since 2004, I have had my students examine the 2004 Global Leadership Compact and its resulting progress. What has continued to concern me is how many organizations did not stay with the initiative, despite enthusiasm in its initial stages. One year, I had students examine the list of organizations that pulled out. Needless to say, that list was long. I cannot help but question why so many decided not to work through the issues, when the issues addressed so many basic needs of our global human communities. Therefore, as I learned from one of my esteemed professors in seminary,

> Modern culture has managed to make itself so blind to the reality of evil that it has become almost incapable of discerning the magnitude of its threat to the human future. How else can we explain the pervasive denial of evil that dominates out time? By turning away from the resources of the mythic imagination, we have stripped ourselves of the capacity to cut through our denial of the destructive forces that we face. (Moore, 2003, p. 9)

Revisiting Privilege

Many studies on organizational identity have been rooted in two schools—the essentialist and the structuralist schools (Czarniawska and Wolff, 1998, p. 35, as cited in Ozen and Kusku, 2009). The essentialist assumption suggests that identity is created by individuals, which sets forth the foundational proposition for some scholars to suggest that organizational identity is the belief and perception of members about their organization's distinctive, central, and enduring characteristics (Albert and Whetten, 1995; Dutton and Dukerich, 1991; Hogg and Terry, 2000, as cited in Ozen and Kusku, 2009). Therefore, the *perceptions* of members regarding their organization's identity can guide their interpretations of strategic issues (Dutton and Dukerich, 1991, as cited in Ozen and Kusku, 2009). Sharma (2000, as cited in Ozen and Kusku, 2009) suggested that managerial interpretations of environmental issues that shape environmental strategies are influenced by the extent to which managers perceive environmental concerns as central to their organization's identity (2009). The structuralist or social constructivist tradition conceptualizes organization identity as shared perceptions among members, whereas the essentialist tradition conceptualizes it as identity-as-institutional claims available to members (Whetten and Mackey, 2002, as cited in Ozen and Kusku, 2009).

So, one may ask, what are the implications of these propositions relative to how organizations may choose to respond to responsible behaviors in less developing countries and/or organizational environments where imbalances in powers exist?

Center stage in both theoretical frameworks are the decisions of the organization's members. Either way, whether the leadership guides the perceived organizational identity or the members assume the organization's preconceived identity, human choices are made by those in power as to the constructs of that identity and resulting actions.

Privilege is said to be most evident when contrasted with its absence (Kravitz, 2002), which may be one explanation as to why people do not want to give up privilege even if giving it up can position them to have more—albeit in the long run. Many who reside within the domains of privilege may neither acknowledge their privilege, nor can or will readily identify with the issues of the underprivileged—doing so brings reality too close to home (2002).

Is it fair to say that privileged groups tend to share a dominant worldview, which *they* have defined and thus see no reason to question (2002)? Along with the sense of normalcy can emerge a sense of superiority, which means that actors who recognize the reality of oppression may become quite uncomfortable because this recognition could imply the possibility of loss of privilege (2002). Therefore, while the major nexus of change may be in one's ability to engage as the "Other," if in doing so you are being brought too close to the reality of their conditions, there will be no seeing that person through their lens.

Are the undertones of these issues any different in our more industrialized environments? Are we doing anything more than taking attitudes and perceptions from one domain to another one, where in both cases there may exist disequilibrium in power? Albeit a rhetorical question—why are we still compelled to make the *business case* for treating people equally and with dignity and respect? What is the value proposition in the reverse, when people employed within the organization—regardless of its domain—do not experience equality? I often ponder how organizations and their respective leaders can actually believe that their organization will prosper in the midst of so much pain felt by their employees.

The plausible outcomes seem simple—the privilege they may desperately hold on to, which positions them to not want to understand their world as it truly exists could be a contributing dynamic to what can eventually cause them to lose privilege. For example, I have often wondered if the same safety training that Union Carbide applied to people in the United States was applied to the workers in Bhopal, India. Was there even a perceived need to train on the same level? I do not have the answers for those rhetorical questions, but I do have my perceptions based upon my being an actor in that environment when the tragedy occurred. However, what I do know was that the outcomes of Bhopal, India not only caused deaths and injury, but also decimated a company that had for many years been a giant in its industry, causing many people in this country to lose their jobs, and for those in power, their privilege.

The research my students have done throughout the years on US-based corporations and other larger industrial nations imposing horrid conditions upon lesser empowered nations raises once again the ugly head of power—inappropriate power. Does the hiring agency have the right to impose inordinate work days, toxic work environments, and crowded conditions, unsafe work conditions, which in our own country would never pass first level OSHA inspections?

For example, there are many debates within the ethics literature grounded in both economic and social responsibility arguments regarding sweatshops. Many debates entertain questions as to whether people in developing countries are better off with or without sweatshops, since they so heavily rely on them to maintain their families. Economic propositions will weigh in on the argument as to whether or not organizational entities will lose some level of profit gain if they increase wages, which might cause other adverse actions such as a decrease in jobs, hence making a case for keeping the wages in the lower economic realms. And from these points the academic and policy arguments expand.

My point is not to argue the economics of running sweatshops. I do believe, however, that as a global society we should question allowing people to work for low wages, for inordinately long hours, within physical and supervisory conditions that would not even remotely withstand scrutiny in the United States and other more highly industrialized societies simply because the people live in abject poverty, need the money, and have no choice.

Unfortunately, as a public, we are asleep at the wheel and, equally sad, we fail to make the connections. I respectfully posit that if the underlying tones are that it is okay to evoke these types of business conditions on poor people of varying hues of color who reside in these countries, what makes you think for a moment that the domestic "worldview" toward difference is going to be any better? Again, revisit the example of Texaco. Their actions in the United States *and* Ecuador speak volumes to this proposition, and they are not the only organization that is guilty of domestic and international travesties.

As a public, we have to take a bigger stance for humanity! How many times have we heard about organizations that support sweatshops, yet we continue to purchase their goods. When my students have studied manufacturers of popular brands of clothing, food, shoes, and so on, and their association with the issues that the United Nations has been addressing since 2004 in the Global Leadership Compact, they can chart little to no public outcry, boycotting, and/ or decreased sales over any length of time in an effort to force an organizational change. Yet, "the time is always right to do what is right" (Martin Luther King Jr.)[8]

Chapter Nine

Transformational Leadership and the Transcendence of Humanity: Leaders Are the Drivers of Change

As our world becomes more complex, the role of leader continues to morph to new levels. Emerging economic, social, and cultural pressures in today's global environment demand that leaders at all levels find better ways to align their vision, core values, and daily actions to produce the needed and valued results at work as well as at home (Friedman and Antal, 2005).

Our continually morphing world calls for *transformational* leaders from all walks of life—business, education, government, social service, NGOs, local communities, and so on. Even in our personal lives, within the domains of our home, we need to have transformational leadership competencies. These are the competencies that progressively and productively move our families forward.

Yet, the process of transformation is bigger than we are and requires a supportive universe (Quinn, 2000). There is a dance of co-creation, but it needs to first start with the self. We begin to awaken to our own simultaneous potential *and* dependence, and we awaken to the sacred potential that is in all living systems (2000). Simply said, moving beyond invoking "managing diversity," or learning to function differently in intercultural environments as well as invoking a much different landscape of employment in developing countries requires moving to a level where each of those actors are seen as sacred human beings with inherent rights no different from the individual driving the process.

All human systems, no matter how secular, are also sacred because they also possess the seeds of transformation. Everyone has the ability to become an agent of change, and we each possess the ability to make a significant contribution to change in ourselves, our relationships, and in any organization or culture we choose to interact with (Quinn, 2000). Therefore, when leaders learn to embrace humanity, they also embrace the opportunity to help this world continually morph to new and far more productive levels—similar in concept to passing forward the baton.

While the constructs of transformational leadership as traditionally defined appear to be simple at face value, they are indeed complex yet attainable. Transformational leaders develop followers into leaders, moving beyond the need to control. They rally people around a mission and vision and awareness of issues, helping people view change from a different lens and set of opportunities (Daft, 2011). Transformational leaders elevate the concerns of followers from lower-level physical needs to higher-level psychological needs such as self-esteem and self-actualization, and they inspire their followers to go beyond their self-interests. Equally important, transformational leaders paint a vision of a desired future state and help their followers understand that this future state is worth the pain of effort that it will take to make the change (2011).

I have addressed the need to recognize humanity and the transcendence of our humanity at varying points in this book. Not until we are able to recognize, value, and love the humanity of each person we come in contact with, even if we do not chose to "like" that person, will we move past the challenges we still have with diversity, intercultural management, and our ability to develop a true egalitarian environment. Until we make that quantum leap, we will still envision managing diversity or invoking new cultural competencies as our only way to understand the varying differences manifested along so many interesting dimensions of our global society

To understand how to embrace humanity from a different lens is to believe that we all are connected to one Source, however, we chose to define that source—whether we call our source God, Allah, Jehovah, or anything else. During my seminary days, I learned that people tend to confuse the constructs associated with religion, theology, and spirituality and as a result will interchangeably use the terms. However, they are very different. What I am speaking to is the oneness of mankind, which is thematically similar along many continuums of spirituality. Hence, we cannot forget how spirituality continues to grow in the management literature. People are continuing to want to link to a higher level of consciousness in this world that can and will evoke more meaning into their lives, relationships, and reasons for being on this earth.

It is not necessary to value people because they share the same religious traditions, or believe that we have to value difference because we are ensconced in the same theological mindset. My point is that we need to value people no matter how different they are from ourselves because we are all spiritually connected to one universe—one source, regardless of the traditions to which we link to and/or identify with.

However, to get to this point is challenging. We are ingrained with many internal barriers that span realms of taught biases, questionable perceptions, and equally critical, imposed limitations that negatively impact our ability to go beyond the walls we build. We become blind to power and domination not only out of a need to expand our material wealth, but also for many other psychological reasons that are associated with our own perceived limitations.

To see people beyond their current immanent or material representations requires a leader who is not afraid to *first* come face to face with his or her shadow self—actions that are absolutely necessary before a leader can assume the role of valuing difference without the prescriptive barriers we have allowed to develop—barriers that are daily becoming more destructive to humanity and our ability to positively interact and uplift one another. Far too many people are despairing, mourning the loss of what we thought we had, bemoaning the state of our democracy, blaming others, and forgetting our own responsibility (Boesak, 2009). A few years ago I was privileged to hear Rev. Allan Boesak, who is also a politician and antiapartheid activist, speak. His words spoke volumes.

> Let us be done with all that now … Yesterday is behind the mist of night. Today is the gift of a new arising. Tomorrow is the dawn of our awakening. The coming days belongs to us! (2009, p. 405)

The time for change is now. However, not until a dedicated group of global leaders emerge—who are willing to truly morph into the role of a transformational leader for *all* of humanity and begin the process of engaging in their own personal transformation in order to move our global society forward—can we eradicate the "isms" that plague our world. So, how do we begin? First and foremost, there are constructs and praxes that committed leaders should visit and challenge.

The concepts and constructs associated with valuing the transcendence of humanity first imply that there is a need to understand and respect people's differences, while at the same time understand that there is a level of equality to which we each are entitled by virtue of our connection to our source. This connection to the universe, to which each of us belongs, privileges the need to go beyond the personalized attributes we "see" when we look at an individual and/or group of people. This connection invites and demands our ability to see people as we see ourselves—as children of our source. It is not our choice or privilege to import relative values upon people, which is why it is so difficult for me to understand the logic (or lack thereof) applied to situating people in circumstances that you, as the person doing the situating would never tolerate.

True transformational leaders need to become aware of the assumptions they tend to make, while also increasing their sensitivity and openness to those who are different from themselves, understanding that there are hidden as well as overt biases that direct one's thinking about individuals, groups, and particular circumstances (Daft, 2008) that will inhibit their ability to connect each person to the overarching connectivity of our universe.

For example, as a transformational leader who values difference, one *must* ask him or herself if he or she would want his or her own children working in a sweatshop. Equally critical, how would he or she feel if his or her daughter applied for a position and was told that because she is a single woman she will be making less money than her male colleague who happens to be married—despite their possessing equal qualifications. Or how would you feel if your spouse was working in a factory and tolling at a 12-hour workday where there are no government regulations regarding work hours? Or, how you would feel as a man of color knowing you make significantly less money than your white counterparts, yet you possess equal to or—push the button further—higher qualifications? Or, that when people look at you, they first look at the color of your skin and not at your character and heart?

As a global society we have to learn to look at people through a different lens, but more importantly, we have to learn to "look" at them. When you look at an individual or group of people different from yourself, you should be honest and ask the question—what are you *choosing* to see?

When attending seminary, one of my courses included a beginning study of Jungian psychology. Jung believed that the well-being of the psyche is directly connected with our conscious or unconscious philosophy of life (Singer, 1994). Our way of looking at things was thought to be of supreme importance to us and our mental health. But, what was interesting was his proposition that the important fact about a situation, thing, (and I am adding person) from a psychological standpoint was not how it objectively looked, but how we *saw* it (1994). Therefore, that which may have previously been unbearable could become acceptable if we made the choice to give up certain prejudices and change our point of view (1994). This philosophy of life could be developed step by step through every increase in experience and knowledge. As a result, a person's image of the world could change as would that person (1994).

To move, however, to that level of transformation, first implies an understanding that the individual should challenge his or her thinking in order to begin a course correction.

Years ago, when I read the works of Dr. Na'im Akbar, this proposition really stood out for me.

> The assumption guiding the traditional paradigms often couched in esoteric and obscure scientific jargon has essentially been: normative reality that is reality characterizing the observations of European descent. Concepts, models methods and modalities, which reaffirm the normality, superiority and legitimacy of this group, are the models, methods and modalities with axiomatic legitimacy within the Western scientific arena. (Akbar, 2003, p. 32)

Self-reflection is critical for leaders who choose to truly emerge as transformational leaders who will move organizations and systems (as well as individuals) toward a new realm of valuing humanity. However, this self-reflection requires challenging current guiding praxes, paradigms, and belief systems.

Human beings are a very special form of creation because we are the only life form that operates based upon a high level of self-consciousness. Therefore, to evoke a change in our behaviors and for the outcomes of those behaviors, we should acquire a consciousness of who we are and what we have been in order to operate to our full human capacity (Akbar, 2003). However, to be successful at this initiative, we should also understand that the Eurocentric attitude of superiority, which drives most of Western thought and impacts or serves as the undergirth of how we function in developing nations, has always been at the expense of building a case for and implementing strategies that drive a perspective of non-Eurocentric inferiority (Akbar, 2003).

To begin a healing and change process, those wanting to truly be transformational change agents for humanity should begin their personal transformational change with a different and more accurate awareness of self, personal history, and contributions in multiple fields, while we concurrently celebrate our life successes (Akbar, 2003). We need to understand and deconstruct the history for what it is—a distorted self-perpetrated rendition of accomplishments that have been obtained at the expense of many cultures of people, which is not a pretty picture—contrary to the one that is typically painted (2003).

Inclusively, when challenging our "self," belief systems and understanding of what constitutes the beauty of humanity, moving away from our own cultural context in order to understand that there already exist cultural contexts that may be far more sophisticated in their basic belief systems of humanity is important.

For example, when attending seminary and further exploring the cultural context of African culture, I marveled at the belief systems of Africans as they pertained to concepts associated with the collective, spirituality, and community, and how morality is an integral part of the education system (Akbar, 1998).

Theirs is a belief that moral teachings emerge from the concept of the soul as the core of the self. Every person learns that they were born to execute a mission toward the advancement of humankind and that each person must seek to identify what that mission might be (1998). Therefore, when teaching the concept of respecting elders, they learn this concept from the perspective of the divine mission each of us have and must come to recognize (1998). Respect for the young by adults emanates from the recognition of a spiritual core or essence in all of us, and the manifestation of that spiritual core is primarily in the service that one renders to the community that you are born into (1998).

Furthermore, the African synthesis of spirituality in the material environment is a lesson that we all can use. You see, in their cultural experience there tends to be no contradiction between their spiritual awareness and their governmental awareness. The two worlds appear to operate quite compatibly so long as the way of approaching the world is rooted in the African view of reality (Akbar, 1998). Yet, altering our behavior to reflect what we really value is revolutionary because principle-driven actions tend to be outside the boundaries of exchange and transaction (Quinn, 2000), which in a Western context tends to define our comfort zones.

From my own Christian context, ten years ago when giving a keynote address, I stated:

> A critical underlying premise is the need for us to be discerners of truth and teach our children to be discerners of truth. Last Sunday our minister reminded our congregation of how the images and metaphors we are faced with daily suggest and even convince some that there are things in life that we cannot do. Messages that the culture sends us that convey the perspective that we do not have options and that we cannot strive to do more. However, he also stressed how Jesus Christ died for us all, not a few, not a select race, not a select age, not a select gender, not a select community, but for every one and inherent in that understanding is that we all have an equal opportunity. Where do we begin to change our paradigms? Where do we begin to get up and challenge the atrocities that continue to plague us? Slavery has already taught us that we are a strong people. So, what is missing? (Easley, 2003)

Through self-celebration, we can heal our damaged self-esteem. It is through the energy of self-worth that humans are motivated to improve and perpetuate themselves. The inspiration for the greatest of human accomplishments in architecture, science, poetry, art, industry, or any other human endeavor has been fueled by the octane of self-worth and a positive self-esteem (Akbar, 1996). Therefore, when leaders who are truly committed to understanding how they can improve the treatment of humanity engage in an appreciative self-assessment, a different level of consciousness can emerge that brings us to a heightened spiritual awareness of who we are, where we come from, and Whose we are.

What can this appreciative self-assessment look like? Transformational leaders are indeed people who are connected (Quinn, 2000). However, learning to become connected is not an "event" that occurs overnight. Growth is key to understanding a basic truth—when we grow, we are in the process of becoming, and during this process we can become fully aligned with our emerging reality (2000). The resources of the universe are attracted to us and we to them, which means as we unfold, we have the ability to take on new levels of complexity (2000). Therefore, reflection upon our journeys of growth and the progress we have thus far made fuels us with the energy to take more positive growth steps. Evaluating and understanding the status of our current relationships, where the positive core of those relationships lie, and how we can take that positive core and move it to new levels is energy provoking.

The decision to move our level of thinking about humanity to a new level, and engage in understanding difference from a different lens also implies humility (Clawson, 2009). It is suggested that since Jim Collins wrote *Good to Great* and introduced his "Level Five Leadership," humility has taken on a new energy in discussions on leadership (2009). Collins focuses on a lack of self-aggrandizement and egocentricity (2009), which I believe is critical to understanding the issues that have been brought forth—particularly one's ability to position oneself in the shoes of those that may be deemed "lesser than." What intrigues me about these issues is that as they have crossed into the management literature, they also reside in the spirituality, theology, as well as psychology of theology literatures. In many of my seminary classes we addressed self-aggrandizement and egocentricity and how destructive it is to our humanity. In other words, across many different realms of thought, people are critically looking at how self-destructive these attributes are to our humanity.

Humility is also important to opening oneself to understanding and embracing the belief that other lands and cultures have figured out very interesting answers to life's problems—which, if one intends to function as an international business person, is a valuable perspective to have (Clawson, 2009).

To sum up my thoughts, I believe Dr. James Clawson's perspective on understanding what it means to be human makes a profound statement:

> By human, I mean that one has a strong sense of his or her membership in the global human community, that we are all more alike than we are different. It goes back to our earlier discussion of geographic differences ranging from human to global region and the like down to the individual. Many if not the vast majority of humans tend to identify more strongly with their local groups and cliques than with the human race. The power of this identification process is manifest in the number of religious, ethnic, racial and other superficial conflicts that continue to rage worldwide. The global business leader may maintain a sense of history, background, and national or ethnic pride; however, their sense of membership in the human group is stronger and dominates their visible behavior. (Clawson, 2009, p. 213)

Chapter Ten

Synthesizing the Learning:
A New Diversity/Intercultural
Competence Model for Change

If we are ever going to change how we view, treat, and inspire people, the change will need to start with people who have leadership roles. And their personal transformation will morph through their respective organizational venues, inspiring the hearts and souls of others to change as well. In our self-transformation, we become a living symbol of change—metaphors that bring about metamorphosis (Chatterjee, 1998, as cited in Quinn, 2004). People who are around us become attracted to our energy in such a manner that they begin to empower themselves—actions that lead to emergent organizing—a change in the system that no one "leads" in the traditional sense (2004).

Let there be no doubt in people's minds; we need a change. Our global society is continually morphing, yet the manner in which we interact with one another has continued to deteriorate.

Throughout the years, as I studied and taught leadership, I became a fan of Dr. Robert Quinn and have required his book, *Deep Change*, as mandatory reading for each of my leadership classes. Dr. Quinn moves the concept of evoking true leadership beyond the concept and construct of "doing" something and pushes the reader to understand that in order to seriously evoke change in our world, we should learn to "be" different. I was blessed to have Dr. Quinn as an instructor in my doctoral program—one of the fundamental experiences I had that never left me.

I believe that if we are to move beyond programmatic initiatives that are designed to evoke "managing" diversity or "gaining" intercultural competence in our world, we have to look to the leaders in our society to begin that change. However, this will require them to be personally challenged at levels they may initially find very uncomfortable.

Deep change within oneself infers a spiritual connection where one can connect with one's purpose (Quinn, 1996). But to do so, people should not be afraid to look at their past—their historical self, and their perspectives of humanity, community, and their oneness with their source.

The failure to personally align before one remotely attempts to step into a venue of authentic leadership where one values humanity is clearly asking for either death by stagnation or death by incompetence. One only has to cite the Enron, WorldCom, and other similar organizations in our world to understand the potential magnitude of outcome. It will take years for our economy and the people who worked for those and similarly situated organizations to recover from the ineptness of the individuals who led those organizations (Robinson-Easley, 2012).

Throughout this book, I loosely define what constitutes an organizational environment. You see, the issues do not just reside within a traditional business context. Across many organizational contexts—traditional organizations, government, communities, countries, and any other form where people are collectively engaged in work and interactions, people are tired of feeling marginalized.

When assessing the value of my propositions, we need to look at the fragile patterns of life. For many who face feeling "less than," these fragile patterns of life are situated within the ongoing process of cultural conversations (Gergen and Thatchenkery, 1996); conversations, belief systems, and historical context that cause significant pain because they are so deeply institutionalized in the realms of racism, which means they are also deeply rooted (Easley, 2010).

People are fundamentally spiritual entities; a distinct presence in this world who clearly have the potential to be the cause of their own actions. Self- development via self-analysis is the catalyst for moving toward change. And, as Dr. Quinn posits (2004), contrary to our assumptions about how leaders create change, deep change at the organizational level is not managed or controlled. It spreads like a contagious disease in a nonlinear fashion. Consequently, to lead transformation is to become a leader of a social movement—which is desperately needed in today's global environment.

So, Where Do We Begin? Step One

The model I have titled "Evoking an Organizational Vision for Valuing Humanity" is a relatively simple model and can be applied to multiple contexts (see figure 10.1). Commitment to bringing forth an organizational climate that values humanity begins with self-reflection and change at the leadership level of an organization, regardless of how organization is defined. The leaders of an organization define the diversity vision and they hold people accountable for driving that vision into every available area of the organization.

However, before engaging in the design, communication, and implementation of a diversity vision, the leadership *must* delve deep inside to understand how they truly feel about humanity and ask the difficult questions.

Are there personally held biases or experiences that can impede the leader clearly articulating a vision for valuing all of humanity? You see, this vision will permeate every aspect of the organization—how it functions domestically as well as in an international environment. I respectfully suggest, for example, that if the leadership has an

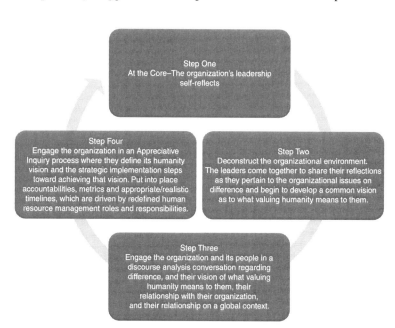

Figure 10.1 Evoking an Organizational Vision for Valuing Humanity.

open heart regarding humanity, there is no way he or she will even remotely entertain the challenges discussed in developing countries, or inappropriate power strategies to prevail in the organization that limit the movement of people who possess many different microcultures. The environment and attitudes toward humanity will be open, free flowing, and embracing.

I do not believe for a moment that any of us are free of some sort of bias. The end result is not to believe something about yourself that may not be true. The ultimate outcome is to recognize where those biases may exist, examine them, find their root causes, and engage in challenging them as well as examine what new paradigms will need to be internalized.

Self-reflection requires the leader sitting down and introspectively examining through meditation, reflection, and self-talk, his or her feelings, actions, and an active engagement of asking hard questions, even if initially those questions are rhetorical. The fact that you articulate the questions is the beginning of a change and healing process.

As our lives grow more complicated, we often find ourselves engaging in behaviors that begin to tear apart our ability to live authentically. It is not until we recognize those behaviors we have internalized for what they are, will we become willing to question them and change.

I have personally found meditating, reading books that I may not have normally picked up, and sitting still in front of my fireplace with the fire going or on the patio with the flowers blooming, opens me to a more in-depth conversation with "me."

I remember a few years ago a friend asked me some very deep questions—the most profound being what would make me "happy." Life had been difficult. I lost my husband to a sudden death—massive heart attack, and my children were going through their own level of pain. As time passed, I found that I continued to hold on to traditions, beliefs, and values that no longer defined me. My life had changed, my children were adults, yet I had not changed. I was no longer married and a mother to growing kids. I was not even sure I wanted to stay in my profession. I simply knew something had to change.

Consequently, when he asked this question, I began to think about the things in my life that gave me joy, and how was I living out of that joy. I also began to reflect on the people whom I had tolerated in relationships—friends, family, colleagues, and so on whose values I no longer shared, but because of our history and my conformity to the past, I had not let go. Although I had traveled internationally for work quite a bit, it was during this time that I began to engage in self-reflection. I traveled more and worked to engage my new international environments beyond what I had done in the past. You know the drill—go to a conference, attend the conference, interact, and then come home. This time I stayed, interacted beyond the professional venues, toured many parts of their lands, and actively engaged the people on a social versus professional basis. My understanding of my world, my worldview, and the possibilities of life morphed to levels that I had not previously envisioned.

So, what I am saying to those leaders who are willing to take on the challenge of change is that there is no set "process" that I believe one has to buy in to. You have to first simply be willing to assume that your paradigms may need adjusting and engage in the questioning process.

Among the many attributes of leadership is the attribute of self-reflection regarding how you, as a leader, view humanity in concert with a lack of fear toward change. When I teach leadership and management, I address with my students the concept of fear. Fear of change is an element we need to be able to move through. That does not mean you aren't fearful—it simply means you have the courage to confront your fears and keep going. Throughout this book, I have touched on the concept of power. I believe many people are afraid of change because they believe that there is an element of power that they will lose. Yet, I also believe that when we let go of "power" in the traditional sense is when we become more powerful. We should learn to let go of those feelings and "things" that bind us and become more willing to reach out and share with others because we do not fear constraint.

Leadership as a foundational quality for emerging through the tumultuousness of today's global environment entails personal, spiritual, and professional growth, and the ability to see the environment for what it is, yet possessing the wisdom to see all plausible scenarios that can emerge while we prepare ourselves for those possibilities (Robinson-Easley, 2013). Yet, everyone who wears the title of leader is not a leader—which is another level of personal confrontation that needs to occur.

Leadership is also about honesty, authenticity, ethical behavior, and, most important, faith—believing that there is something higher than you to call upon. In other words, leadership is about what is inside you, which is why understanding how you interact with and process your social context is so important (Robinson-Easley, 2013). I have also found that an active engagement in the spirituality literature is very helpful as we begin to frame our personal questions. To change circumstances means starting with an examination of self, which requires significant leadership competencies. Many people are prisoners of paradigmatic blockages and as a result refuse to even think about change (Robinson-Easley, 2013). Focused and committed leaders who understand that they must first challenge their praxes, paradigms, and internalized beliefs regarding difference are thrust center stage, facing what makes them who they are.

In doing so, we have to be willing to step outside ourselves and embrace *disconfirming* feedback, see and hear unpleasant things about ourselves and understand growth as a process (Quinn, Spreitzer, and Brown, 2000; Robinson-Easley, 2013). Successfully altering the human system is a critical part of adaptive change where needed expertise and tools do not already exist. Real change will therefore require people to make very painful adjustments in their attitudes, work habits, and lives (Quinn, Spreitzer, and Brown, 2000).

When we work to evoke change in our lives, an important step is to incorporate appreciation when we examine our past—a concept that bears repeating. Yet, we should also turn inward and examine the potential for self-hypocrisy, which requires personal discipline to cope with the pain involved in examining your integrity gaps in order to change behavior (Quinn, Spreitzer, and Brown, 2000).

Quinn, Spreitzer, and Brown (2000), discuss Torbert's proposition that people (particularly professionals) will perform well as long as their assumptions about the situation are not violated (Robinson-Easley, 2013). Yet, they also present Torbert's proposition that it is possible to deviate from the norm through an awakened attention that allows you to press forward in uncertain and threatening situations, learning as you go—an activity he calls action inquiry (Torbert, 1987, as cited in Quinn, Spreitzer, and Brown, 2000) Leaders need to be open to reframing how they view a situation, as they consciously seek and choose new frames to ensure that their behavior is aligned with key values—actions that keep the change agent in a process of self-creating and self-transfiguring (2000).

In a previous publication, I tell the story of my interaction with Dr. William (Bill) Torbert, and I think the story is worth retelling in this book.

I had Drs. Torbert and Quinn as professors in my doctoral program and found each to be ahead of their time. I never will forget how Bill required our class to engage in an autobiographical writing assignment that required us to deconstruct our behaviors on many different continuums (Robinson-Easley, 2013). I protested in more ways than one could imagine—simply because I did not want to confront the "decay" that Quinn describes. Yet, Bill was quite adamant and simply stated that if I wanted to pass his class, I would write the assignment (2013).

Not quite a year later, I had the opportunity to see Bill again at a conference in Stroud, England, where 65 participants lived under one roof, studied, and engaged in lively exchanges for several days (2013). Despite my writing the assignment from an initial mindset of protest, I had to admit to Bill while we were in England that it was the best thing I had done in recent years (2013). You see, I learned through that assignment that as Quinn, Spreitzer, and Brown so appropriately suggest, you cannot change others (and I am going to take the liberty to add—or your environment) until you have made the painful adjustments by surrendering and placing yourself in jeopardy as you work to become part of an emergent system (2000).

Quinn, Spreitzer, and Brown also suggest through a perusal of Dr. Peter Reason's work (who led the Stroud conference and also was ahead of his time) that leaders of change must be open to reframing how they view a situation, as they consciously seek and choose new frames to ensure that their behavior is aligned with key values— actions that keep the change agent in a process of self-creating and self-transfiguring (2000).

Our global world is an emergent system; it is continually morphing. Being open to engaging in change to adequately meet the requirements of this emergent system also calls for surrendering to your ability to tolerate uncertainty while you engage in strategies that will help you develop your new steps (Robinson-Easley, 2013). Yes, this change will definitely be discontinuous, radical, and painful

(Quinn, Spreitzer, and Brown, 2000). Yet, the outcome can far exceed what we ever expected from ourselves (Robinson-Easley, 2013).

Beginning the Morphing Process: Step Two—the Engagement of Other Leaders

It is not enough for one leader to go through this self-reflection process. Each leader in the organization (again, however we choose to define organization) should engage in their individual processes. Yet, once achieved (and the time frame allocated should allow for a natural process to emerge), it is then time for the leaders to collectively come together to share their insights.

By sharing insights, it is important for them to share their perceptions of how meaning occurs within the organization; the praxes and assumptions they believe have impacted how the organization views difference and the personal challenges to organizational behaviors they have allowed that may impact the organization's ability to move valuing humanity to a different level.

It is also important that the leaders deconstruct the organizational *behaviors* and how they have been allowed to develop, evaluating the discourses that exist in the organization and how they perceive messages are interpreted. It is important to thematically map these discourses because they will tend to impact the organization's culture, which is the next topic for discussion. Leaders and their teams need to talk about the culture of the organization—its personality and the perceptions of how difference is valued. They should talk through their personal perceptions of how the organization's culture is defined and encouraged, what communication patterns exist or do not exist, and, equally important, what are the venues in which power is allowed to evolve.

The concepts of organizational power and personal power should also be discussed from a very different perspective. Power as a concept is very complex. There are many power games played in organizations by people who have absolutely no vested interest in the outcomes relative to the lives of people involved with the organization (Robinson-Easley, 2012).

People become pawns in their games.

Yet, far too many times the organization is enamored by these people because of their ability to exert charismatic power. Far too often, we do not take the time to discern who the power brokers are and their real motives (2012). Yet, when our change processes begin, we have to put on the lens of discernment in order to avoid their blocking efforts. Power strategies, in any venue, always have been and always will continue to be dualistic (2012). In many ways, power strategies can help drive change at a rapid pace because the right brokers are in place. However, on the flip side, if not understood and equally managed, power strategies in the wrong hands can derail a noble cause (2012).

I have taught power strategies as a class for over ten years. One of the first exercises I ask students to do is to identify the organizational chart of their particular business context. On that chart, I ask them to identify those people who are allegedly in power by virtue of title and position (2012). Next, I ask them to identify who the "real" power brokers are in their organizations and develop the shadow organizational chart. Over the past ten-plus years I have conducted this exercise, inevitably 80 percent of the students see that the organizational chart that theoretically represents who is in power is antithetical to the "real" organizational chart that identifies where the "true" power lies in the organization (2012). And, equally disturbing, the majority of the students, albeit antidotal examples, can cite how these unofficial power brokers have had negative impact upon the organization, actions that left them wondering how strong were the people who officially were represented on the organizational chart.

As we begin to invoke true change within our organizations, understanding the dynamics of power and its intersection with and relationship to other organizational systems are critical concepts for us to deconstruct. Far too often, what we see in front of us is not "real." Generally, it is within the shadows where the real issues as well as those with whom we interact lie (2012). Therefore, when we look at the real reasons why sweatshops occur, child labor issues emerge, women are treated less than men, and the list can go on, the organization's leadership needs to adequately deconstruct the dynamics of power and perceived privilege at all levels within the organizational structure. They also need to have authentic conversations as to what are the alternative paradigms of more socially appropriate behaviors and how those behaviors can and will uplift people. And, equally critical, they should have authentic conversations as to why they personally have allowed these dynamics to exist. In other words, at what point during their leadership did they abdicate their power, and more importantly—why?

Once these conversations emerge and continue, and again I suggest allowing sufficient time for them to morph—in other words do not encourage these conversations to be an "event"—then it is important for the leadership to move to the next step, which is developing what they would like to see as a humanity vision. However, they should also understand that before the organization embarks upon a humanity vision, there is additional feedback needed—that of the organization's. Yet, before moving to that step, it is important for them to determine that each leader is in fact on the same page with regard to forward movement.

Step Three—Engaging the Organization

The third step in the model suggests engaging the organization in a dialogue that explores their concept of humanity, their treatment within the organization and overall how they view the organization with respect to how it values humanity. In other words, they need to express how they see the organization constructing its reality.

However, even within the constructivist view, there is a tendency to adopt a structural-functionalist view in which the job of change is to align, fit, or adapt organizations, through interventions, to an objective reality that exist "out there" (Ford, 1999). This is not what I advocate, simply because it similarly represents the approaches defined in previous chapters that have failed to yield true change.

Organizations exist as socially constructed realities in which the reality we know is interpreted, constructed, enacted, and maintained through discourse (Beter and Luckmann, 1966; Holzner, 1972; Searle, 1995; Watzlawick, 1984a; and Weick, 1979, as cited in Ford, 1999). In such a constructivist view, change agents would then use interventions not to bring about a greater alignment with a "true" reality, but construct, deconstruct, and reconstruct existing realities so as to bring about another type of performance(s) (Ford, 1999).

Within a conversational context, organizations can be understood as many networks of conversations that construct multiple realities. These conversations provide the texture of the organization and are pluralistic and polyphonic in nature with many conversations occurring simultaneously and sequentially (Fairclough, 1992; Haze, 1993, as cited in Ford, 1999).

These conversations can construct and *produce* change; therefore the intervention of change is in fact the conversation. Therefore, change agents use conversations to bring about alterations in some nonlinguistic internal human state or environmental state, which produces a different, yet intentionally desired outcome (Ford, 1999).

The conversations that the leader has with himself and subsequently with his other leadership team members is in fact the first step in invoking a change process—you become conscious of the need for and importance of a different dialogue to set forth a new organizational context. Therefore, if humanity is reconstructed to view all people on a level playing field, the resulting actions toward individuals will be different with respect to its linguistic construction and resulting actions.

The Contextual Framework of a Double Loop Model and Its Importance to the Model

As previously discussed, Dr. Alvarez and I began developing an alternative change model that incorporated the theory and practice of Discourse Analysis *and* AI. Our model suggested that the complementary dynamics between these two approaches via a double loop process would serve to bring forth those hidden representations at a deep discursive level while at the same time working to help participants understand, through a reconstruction process, the associated meanings that emerge (Robinson-Easley, 2012).

Our initial proposition was to first deconstruct the ensuing language in order to understand how to reconstruct a new language. Once participants better understood the feelings and emotions they deeply buried and their associated metaphors, it would be much easier to move forward in a change process (2012). What was missing in the model however, was the deep discursive actions of the leadership. To drive the type of change that is needed in our diversity dialogues requires those that lead to embrace the change first. The simplicity of having a diversity "vision" is not enough. Unless you can live that vision, articulate it naturally in all you say and do, it becomes nothing more than a symbol of what should be versus what is, in the present and future—enacted by those at the top.

Therefore, gathering organizational members together in a whole-system venue is an important next step, but not before the two steps that engage the leadership. They have to first provide their input and speak into their perceptions as to how they see, feel, and believe the organization values humanity. If the leadership has authentically engaged in this process, as defined in the first and second steps of the model, they will convey through their discourse, as well as nonverbal cues, their receptivity to the organizational members' input. In other words, they will not be as quick to dismiss their "truths," but will work toward engaging in a deep listening process in order to better understand.

Change, however, is not built around one dialogue. Rather it can be viewed as a polyphonic phenomenon, where stories are built within stories, themes within conversations are introduced, maintained, and deleted (Ford, 1999). Therefore, movement through the double loop process Dr. Alvarez and I introduced can provide the organization with the opportunity to obtain significant information regarding the culture and microcultures of the participants, their values and beliefs, in concert with their critical perceptions of the organization and its ability to value humanity (Robinson-Easley, 2012; Easley and Alvarez-Pompilius, 2003).

It is also important to note that if the size of the organization prohibits bringing everyone together at one time in one venue, there are organization development strategies within the overarching concept of whole-systems change that can help the organization evoke movement through smaller group sessions and collaborative communication processes, where feedback and engagement is still accomplished, which means there is no reason not to involve the "system."

During this stage it is imperative that someone is charged with the responsibility to capture key points of all conversations. Search conference methodology is a wonderful way to engage the whole system. Yet, the gatherings should be emergent and allowed to flow as necessary. Captured data should be reflected upon, allowing people time to reflect and come back to engage in more dialogue regarding their reflections.

Yes, this is time consuming, and yes, it can cost the organization dollars, but if we are continually pressed to make the "business case," I respectfully suggest that the human resource function be charged with the responsibility to do the analysis of how the failure to value difference has thus far cost the organization.

What are issues of turnover and their associated costs, absenteeism, poor quality production, increased medical insurance rates, and all other metrics associated with human capital valuation? And if the organization operates on a global level, what is its reputation in developing countries? While it may be "painful" initially taking time and resources to engage in this type of reflective/reflexive process, I am sure the numbers that reflect upon the negative aspects of how human capital is managed will support both the time and allotted financial resources.

Those engaged in dialogue must be able to step back and critically examine the *themes* that emerge (Robinson-Easley, 2012). This analytical process is critical and serves as a higher-level understanding of the ensuing organizational dialogues and their impact upon the organization's culture and other behavioral patterns (e.g. communications, power dynamics, interaction with leaders and managers, etc.) If the participants are open as well as honest with themselves and their colleagues engaged in this process, a wealth of information will emerge (2012).

By the time the participants engage in the second stage of *change*, where they would have exchanged (deconstructed and analyzed) on the knowledge created, they emerge better equipped to move through an appreciative process and fully internalize and appreciate their strengths and opportunities in order to evoke new visions and design the associated strategic processes (Easley and Alvarez-Pompilius, 2003).

It is during this appreciative process that it becomes important for the organization and its leaders to envision how the organization can morph to new levels with respect to how it values humanity, simply because the dialogue shifts to identifying the positive core of the organization, through storytelling where there have been successes. Even in dire situations, we have to believe that something good has occurred. It is those kernels of goodness that give hope that the organization can indeed move forward. So, for example, if this dialogue were to develop within the context of a sweatshop, perhaps the kernel of goodness would be examining how the opportunity to work has helped change the lives of the workers, still leaving room to understand where opportunities for positive change exist from the lens of the leaders as well as workers.

During this process, it is critical for the organization to insist on a new dialogue regarding humanity and identify the strategies that they each will commit to putting into place to insure that this new dialogue remains a constant one within the organization. The application of discourse analysis serves as both a catalyst and process for helping participants deconstruct their issues in order to understand the overt as well as hidden linguistic representations of their interactions with themselves and their environment (Robinson-Easley, 2012). It provides the overarching venue to understand the organization's performance with regard to difference and their reactive responses to the organization.

AI serves as both a catalyst for evoking a new language based upon the praxis and principles of AI as well as a healing and reconciliation process, which allows organizational members to move forward with an internalized process where they accept their accomplishments and competencies/strengths (Robinson-Easley, 2012). Proponents of AI might argue that engaging in a conversation that in essence dredges up negative images and feelings is counter to the productive and positive components of AI. Yet,

> as a people who have so frequently been victimized by lies—scholarly, pseudo-scientific, and otherwise—we want to be as sure as we can that we are "speaking the truth," to borrow the title of one of James H. Cone's books. But we ought to also be sure that speaking the truth depends on first seeking the truth, then knowing the truth, and finally, and indispensably, doing the truth. (Wilmore, 2007, p. 77, as cited in Robinson-Easley, 2012)

Our worldviews have to be compared and contrasted to the individuality of our experiences versus other subjects who remotely do not share our experiences or understand how we internalize our reality (Robinson-Easley, 2012). Or as Anzaldúa profoundly stated,

> At some point, on our way to a new consciousness, we will have to leave the opposite bank, the split between the two mortal combatants somehow healed so that we are on both shores at once and, at once, see through serpent and eagle eyes. Or perhaps we will

disengage from the dominant culture, write it off altogether as a lost cause, and cross the border into a wholly new and separate territory. Or we might go another route. The possibilities are numerous once we decide to act and not react. (Anzaldúa, 2007, p. 101)

To first move to an appreciative conversation and assume that we can consistently deconstruct our experiences within a context of appreciation while we are playing back in our minds the various "isms" and attacks on our psyche, may be naïve (Robinson-Easley, 2012). This was the underlying flaw, I believe, in assuming AI would work in the organization that underwent a consent decree that required their engaging in training 1000 members of their organization. However, in light of other training modalities and the organization's refusal to consider anything but the mandated training, it was by far the best option. Yet, for organizations that are looking to move to the next level relative to how they value humanity, the multiple steps identified in figure 10.1 are critical. You cannot compromise the process for the sake of saving time if you are looking to evoke real change in your organization.

People who feel oppressed in multiple organizational venues are the cumulative by-products of *sustained* oppression. Consider the possibility that the only meaningful approach to helping them understand their feelings in concert with helping the organization understand its behaviors is from the perspective of allowing them to engage in identifying the venues in which they see themselves being oppressed (Akbar, 2003). Therefore, the discourse analysis component of this double loop process is believed to be vital to understanding how one can move to a healing and appreciative state of being.

Understanding the Etiology of Discourse Analysis

A view of discourse that I believe is more appropriate when used in environments where people have incurred oppression is that it is not just a linguistic device, but central to how people construct their reality (Berger and Luckmann, 1967, as cited in Oswick, Keenoy, and Grant, 2000). There are many layers of "reality" that people who face "isms" have internalized, and if we carefully listen, these realities do play out in our language (Robinson-Easley, 2012).

The various ways in which language mediates between the world and perceptions of the world are primary loci of analysis, thereby suggesting that styles of discourse be examined as they played roles in the gathering and analysis of field data (Manning, 1979).

Discourse has "determining capacities" and when tied to social relations, identities, power, culture, and social struggle, is believed to produce a particular version of social reality (Alvesson and Karreman, 2000; Chia, 2000). Discourses from the past can and do shape present and future behavior in the form of established societal beliefs, theories, and stories (Marshak and Grant, 2008). Consequently, when we view discourse as central to the social construction of reality (Berger and Luckmann, 1967, as cited in Oswick, Keenoy, and Grant, 2000), we position ourselves to better understand how inequalities in power determine one's perceived ability to control the production, distribution, and consumption of particular language texts (Oswick, Keenoy, and Grant, 2000); a perspective that is quite informing and critical to behavioral scientists working to evoke change in challenged and/or marginalized communities and/or organizations (Easley, 2011).

These language patterns structurally include central themes, root or generative metaphors well as rhetorical strategies (Kets de Vries and Miller, 1987; Thatchenkery, 1996; Hopkins and Reicher, 1997). This is critical information for organizational leaders as well as their respective workers to know and understand. You see, it is these generative metaphors and how we have given them power over our lives that are critical underlays to how we construct our reality. If concepts and language are sufficiently reinforced, they will become internalized beliefs (Robinson-Easley, 2012).

What potentially can emerge in these conversations are the workers' own internalized belief systems that emerge from how they have learned to perceive their environment. What the organization can learn is the perceived "truth" their employees have internalized regarding the organization and its respective leaders, which may not be grounded in intended actions, but coexists with other internalized discourses from people's past and present constructed realities.

When both organizational members and their leaders engage in a conversation that invites a deconstructive analysis that closely examines cultural sensitivity to language, an added benefit occurs—they have the ability to evoke a comprehensive understanding of their cultural realms and how it informs their reality, which becomes a unique education process (Robinson-Easley, 2012). I believe the downside of sensitivity training years ago was that there was no attempt to thematically analyze the discourse. The discourse was deconstructed in a manner that evoked a dichotomous either/or scenario. Either you were a racist or sexist, or you weren't. Consequently, there were many lines drawn in the "sand" and a lot of backlash when people returned to their respective organizations.

A sound facilitation process built into the discourse analysis can begin to break down defense mechanisms and help participants better understand their origins (Robinson-Easley, 2012). Self-knowledge is critical to one's ability to evoke deep change. Building a thematic analysis of the overarching themes that emerge from our language will also provide us with informing knowledge of behavioral patterns, thereby enabling us to correct those behaviors because we see their relational values.

When the conversation shifts, they shift what people pay attention to and talk about. Shifting conversations also opens space for new actions and results to occur. When looking to evoke change, first understand the existing network of conversations and then proceed to add, weed out, supplement, reintegrate, and organize conversations in order to construct a reality that fits together with coherence and integrity, and supports further exploration and invention (Schwandt, 1994, as cited in Ford, 1999).

I strongly believe that deconstructing, thematically analyzing and sharing information relative to our discourse is indeed the *core* of the change process. Through disclosed patterns of discourse, we can understand the relational bonds that exist between people, and how structure is created, transformed, and maintained. Through the study of discourse as a change process, we reinforce or challenge our beliefs (Barrett, Thomas, Hocevar, 1995). Challenging beliefs is a critical action if an organization is to move toward an ability to value humanity. Challenging beliefs is critical to the first and second steps of the process where the leaders engage in their initial private, then collective discourses. It is through the challenge of those belief systems that one can grow. Producing organizational change requires a type of language shift (Holmes, 1992, as cited in Ford,

1999) that produces an attractive and empowering reality (Block, 1987; Ford and Ford, 1994, as cited in Ford, 1999). Equally important, the movement from a monologue to a dialogue adds power to the investigative processes of underlying assumptions and certainties that inform everyday experiences (Ford, 1999).

I will add another benefit to the concept of discourse analysis. When we obtain sacred space to have these critical conversations, we have the privacy to dislodge the rage that has been suppressed in us for far too many years (Robinson-Easley, 2012), a necessary action if we are to engage in healing.

This is a hard process. I still remember my reactions to the late President Nelson Mandela's call for reconciliation in South Africa. I pondered from many contexts whether or not I could go through "real" inner reconciliation had I lived in South Africa and under the oppression of apartheid. Yet, there is no doubt in my mind that this country needed to heal and I believe that their engagement in this process significantly helped the people and the country of South Africa move forward.

I also understand that if we are to change our world and remove the variations of "isms" that exist, we have to let go of the rage. I cannot, however, reiterate too much how important are the deconstruction and analytical processes of discourse analysis. It is not enough to engage in the dialogue (Robinson-Easley, 2012). We need to closely and critically examine the themes that emerge and correlate them to the root metaphors that reinforce their existence. It is not until we engage in this level of analysis can we truly begin to diminish the power they hold over our social context (Robinson-Easley, 2012).

The Last Steps of the Model

Co-constructing a new vision for the organization as an outcome of the AI process, which is the second stage of the double loop model, is important. The AI process positions participants to discover where they have been at their best by sharing stories. There is a significant value in organizational storytelling. For one, it allows a very basic opportunity to hear what is important to colleagues—actions and events that you may not have even been aware of. It is also at this stage that the language shift begins moving toward a common vision of change.

Inherent in the AI process is also a strategic planning component, where people are encouraged to dream the ideal state for their organization and, I also add, relationships. This stage of change invites excitement, and a realization that through noninvasive, nonprogrammatic shifts (e.g. via just the beginning of changing one's language), change is inevitable. It also facilitates the opportunity for the leaders and organizational members to co-construct their vision, and it allows the organizational leaders the opportunity to validate if where they thought the vision for change should lie is indeed relevant for their people. In other words, this process will help the organization's leadership team validate if they are even close to understanding the heartbeats of their people.

Through the combination of these two methodologies as we have outlined in our double loop process, a different type of bonding and awareness can occur. Sensitivity training years ago tried to accomplish this via reconciliation processes. But the processes did not heal, they only promoted a lot of anger in people because they were not allowed to "see" and hear about their peak experiences where they have already shown that they have the potential to reach their new vision.

Inherent in this phase of change is an emphasis on strategy and implementation, which are very important processes. Those steps cannot be shortchanged because if they are, the organization will risk losing momentum and once again morph into an "event" and/or process. Emphasis on designing strategy and implementation steps is important. The learning that the leaders have gleaned from the prior training will be germane at this stage. They will better understand the differences between strategic goals, tactical steps, and project management strategies for staying on target. And, also germane to making this work is importing accountability measures into the strategic and tactical steps.

You see, where organizations of many venues have typically broken down in their drive toward change is in this phase of the process. Realignment initiatives and forward moving action over and above doing one's daily job can be draining if not correctly managed. Therefore, the organizational leaders have to insure that they have team(s) of people in place dedicated to insuring that the change processes are on target. The downside of not doing so is the loss of credibility with your organizational members, who will see these failures as a movement toward "back to business as usual." That is a fate that no organizational leadership team wants to experience. Therefore implementation cannot be shortchanged. And if there are any tendencies to believe that these actions cannot be effectively accomplished, once again I suggest you go back to the business case your human resource management personnel will make. The real question is, can you afford not to engage in change?

The final stage of AI is, setting forth a destiny where change is sustained. This stage and resulting dialogues are critical for organizations looking to embrace humanity. Sustaining the change is the only way we will be able to keep us developing with a global mindset (Robinson-Easley, 2012).

A Critical Step in the Last Stage of the Model—Redefining the Role of the Human Resource Professional to Institutionalize the Change

Throughout this book, I have made numerous references to the issues that plague human resource professionals when looking to evoke diversity and/or intercultural management change. Human Resource professionals have a very important position in designing and implementing strategies within their organization that are focused on moving the organization toward a culture that values humanity. In many respects they are seen as the drivers of change. Yet, it is very hard for human resource professionals to drive change in the absence of the organization's key and critical actors initiating a change process, which is why the initial steps of the proposed model begin at the top of the organization and result in a whole-systems change process that drives consensus as to what constitutes valuing humanity in the organization.

Given the widespread impact of globalization and internationalization, workplace diversity is now a fact of life that is going to continue (Okoro and Washington, 2012). Yet, it truly is up to the organization's leadership as to how serious the organization is with reference to inculcating it into the core of the organization. But in the midst of organizations making up their minds regarding their position on diversity, current trends in domestic and global workplaces clearly indicate the need for intercultural competence within an organization (2012).

While there is a consensus that organizations must do something different on a global context relative to their ability to value humanity, the real question is, where is the responsibility for institutionalizing the change that is posited in the model.

Over the course of the years that I have worked in human resources as well as taught strategic human resource management to mid- and senior-level executives, the one constant I have learned is that human resource strategies do not alone drive *and* sustain the change an organization may be looking for. However, the elements within the proposed model are designed to evoke an organizational change that has the potential to alter critical behaviors within the organization—the leadership, communications, power dynamics, organizational (personality) culture, in addition to, most important, how the organization values the differences that lies within its workforce.

As previously noted, accountability measures and the identification of individuals within the organization that will bear the accountability is critical. Yet, concomitant to the implementation/accountability processes should lie the human resource programmatic initiatives that have the ability to institutionalize the change.

Consequently, the ability to identify the critical core competencies that will be needed to continue the changed culture will be the responsibility of human resources in addition to designing and implementing recruitment and retention strategies that will insure people staying within the organization. Ongoing training and development that helps further an understanding of intercultural competence and other requisite skills needed by the organization also becomes the responsibility of the human resource professional.

The role of the human resource professional at this juncture is very critical. The human resource department becomes the linchpin for insuring that these initiatives and the energy that has been afforded to them are not in vain. Human Resources will also have the responsibility for integrating all resources into an appropriate human capital strategy that requires their human resource professionals to expand beyond the traditional role of HR.

The human resources department can breathe life into a failing system and insure that there is an active integration of members of the workforce (duPlessis, 2012).

The Value Proposition of This Model

First and foremost, let me be clear as to why the model is written in a circular format (figure 10.1). This design is intentional. The arrows suggest that once the processes are complete they start over again. One can never grow comfortable in praxes and assumptions, particularly as our global environment changes. Therefore, once the organization has completed the cycle, at some point in time the process should be repeated. The rationale for doing so is simple. Our global environment continues to morph and change. Nothing is static. Consequently, we should never assume that our guiding praxes will remain static. I am not suggesting that you immediately reengage the model, but at a respectable point in time the organization and its leaders (who can also change as time lapses) will grow as will the global diversity environment.

This model does not embrace programs, it does not embrace hiring people, and it does not embrace looking at quotas or management/employee development strategies, or training of any sort. What this model embraces is people sitting down and talking with one another about their feelings, their dreams, their desires, and their concerns. Constructive conversations ensue that have the potential to remove barriers and bond people from a different level of consciousness.

You see, you can hire all the new people in the organization you want, invoke all the diversity statements and handbook documents and engage in any and all other types of structural change. But, what I suggest to you is nothing is more powerful than hearing the human heart.

As I was writing, I was still reflecting upon the strife that was occurring in Turkey and Egypt. So many assumptions are being made about how the people feel. People need to "hear" how another feels, and not in a venue of protest. They need to hear where others feel marginalized and leaders should go inside themselves and ask the hard questions.

I sincerely believe that when we move away from hiding behind inappropriate uses of power, politics, and—yes, I am going to say it—human resource strategies that do not get to the heart of the matter, we will truly begin to carve out a world that values humanity.

The components of the model I have identified are not difficult if there is a commitment to heal the hearts and souls of our world. The tough part is simply putting aside our varying levels of egos and understanding that there may be something new we need to hear and learn from one another. We can no longer afford to assume how people see their world and live in it, and quite frankly we can no longer afford to marginalize people.

In so many industrialized countries, we are losing ground on multiple realms simply because there is such an erosion of classes due to policies and decisions that do not take into account the humanity of the people they represent.

Yet, I believe in humanity and more importantly I believe in our ability to change. I also believe that there are enough people out here to form a critical mass of people that want to change our world. They just need to know how. I also believe that once organizational leaders begin a change process and experience the change, others will follow. Yet, there needs to be a start.

Individuals have the power to do the same with the model on smaller scales. As an individual, you can begin to evoke a change, via the components of the model, by simply engaging people and, more importantly, the "self" in venues where you have influence and input. Leadership is not defined by the size of your organization or the scope of your authority. True leaders, no matter where they reside—whether in a corporate board room, heading up a little league baseball team, or heading a church ministry—will appreciate, understand, and value the individual threads that make up our vast "oneness." The phenomenal writer Maya Angelou concretizes this concept best when she says, "We all should know that diversity makes for a rich tapestry, and we must understand that all the threads of the tapestry are equal in value no matter what their color."[1] Our world has so much potential; we already are a vast and rich tapestry that has the ability to evoke more wonders than we can begin to imagine. Just think what could happen when people feel totally free to be themselves; knowing and believing that they are valued for their individualities.

I often tell my students when they become frustrated when looking at how much change is needed either within their organizations or in our world, that all they have to do is throw one pebble into a pond and see the ripples eventually turn into waves. And, I also challenge organizational leaders to do the same—you have the power, the platform, and the audience to begin a movement toward valuing humanity that has the potential to eliminate the need for literatures to address the multiple issues of "isms" identified in this book and others. One pebble in the water at a time, or as posited centuries ago, "The journey of a thousand miles begins with a single step."[2] Yet, if the leaders of our world begin that *single* step, our journey toward *valuing humanity* can be a much shorter journey than the one we embarked upon when we began to invoke our varying civil rights laws across many different countries and varied diversity training forums.

In Closing

As I was coming close to finishing this book, what kept playing in my head and heart was the phrase "what do you see when you look at me?" I wonder if that is what people think as they engage difference. What do we see? Can we see beyond the physical differences and into the hearts and souls of people? Can we look at others as equals in this vast domain of humanity because they are equally connected to one universe and move past the need to manage difference at any level? Can we put the various regulatory agencies out of work and utilize their talents for something far more productive in today's global work versus policing behavior?

I believe that if challenged to look at how we have constructed our world, a vast majority of people will change. Yet, I believe that people have to be challenged to grow uncomfortable in their paradigms.

Therefore, I hope I have provided that challenge and beginning options for change. If nothing more, I pray that by reading this book, you engage in a different, provocative, and productive dialogue that moves you and others toward the real process of valuing humanity. Individually, everyone has a role and responsibility to make a difference in our thinking about difference. You see, as Robert F. Kennedy suggested, "Each time someone stands up for an ideal, or acts to improve the lot of others, or strikes out against injustice, he (she) sends forth a tiny ripple of hope."[3] Let each of us embrace hope in concert with positive change—today. Our global village is counting on us!

Notes

Preface

1. Mahatma Gandhi quote, http://www.goodreads.com/quotes/54375-love -is-the-strongest-force-the-world-possesses-and-yet, downloaded May 6, 2013.
2. http://www.heartsandminds.org/quotes/effort.htm.

Introduction

1. Rev. Michael L Pfleger speaking engagement at Governors State University on June 4, 2013, at 6:30 pm, University Park, Illinois.
2. Rev. Michael L. Pfleger speaking engagement at Governors State University on June 4, 2013, at 6:30 pm, University Park, Illinois.
3. Rev. Dr. Martin Luther King Jr. http://mlk-kpp01.stanford.edu/index .php/encyclopedia/documentsentry/annotated_letter_from_birmingham/, downloaded May 6, 2013.
4. http://www.heartsandminds.org/quotes/change.htm.

1   Understanding Diversity from the Mindset of a Structural Approach to Change

1. Richard Henry Dana Jr., http://www.goodreads.com/author/quotes/192314 .Richard_Henry_Dana_Jr_, downloaded 5/6/2013.

4   The Importance of the Individual When Working to Evoke a Diverse Organizational Environment

1. http://www.thefreedictionary.com/Othering.
2. Maya Angelou, http://thinkexist.com/quotation/while_I_know_myself _as_a_creation_of_god-I_am/344573.html, downloaded May 6, 2013.
3. http://www.heartsandminds.org/quotes/love.htm.
4. Ecumenical definition cited from http://www.wordnik.com/words /ecumenical.

5 Contemporary, Yet Unconventional Research and Perspectives on Issues of Diversity and Intercultural Management

1. http://www.merriam-webster.com/dictionary/geopolitics.
2. http://en.wikipedia.org/wiki/Geopolitics.
3. http://en.wikipedia.org/wiki/Geopolitics.
4. http://en.wikipedia.org/wiki/Turkey.
5. http://en.wikipedia.org/wiki/Turkey.
6. http://news.bbc.co.uk/2/hi/europe/country_profiles/1022222.stm.

8 Moving the Conversation beyond the Ethics Literature: Connecting Diversity and Social Responsibility

1. Rev. Dr. Martin Luther King Jr. http://www.brighthubeducation.com /history-homework-help/88990-figurative-language-and-metaphors-in-i -have-a-dream-speech/, downloaded 5/6/2013.
2. http://www.umich.edu/~snre492/Jones/texaco.htm.
3. http://www.nytimes.com/1996/11/06/opinion/racism-at-texaco.html.
4. http://www.unglobalcompact.org/NewsAndEvents/event_archives /global_compact_leaders_summit.html.
5. http://www.unglobalcompact.org/AboutTheGC/TheTenPrinciples/index .html.
6. http://www.unglobalcompact.org/Issues/human_rights/equality_means _business.html.
7. http://www.unglobalcompact.org/Issues/human_rights/equality_means _business.html.
8. http://www.heartsandminds.org/quotes/ethics.htm.

11 Concluding Comments

1. http://www.goodreads.com/quotes/67256-we-all-should-know-that -diversity-makes-for-a-rich.
2. Lao Tzu, http://www.quotationspage.com/quote/24004.html, downloaded 3/27/2013.
3. http://www.heartsandminds.org/quotes/lead.htm.

Bibliography

Akbar, N. (1996). *Breaking the Chains of Psychological Slavery*. Tallahassee, FL: Mind Productions and Associates.

Akbar, N. (1998). *Know Thy Self*. Tallahassee, FL: Mind Productions and Associates.

Akbar, N. (2003). *Akbar Papers in African Psychology*. Tallahassee, FL: Mind Productions and Associates.

Allen, D. and P. Hardin. (2001). "Discourse Analysis and the Epidemiology of Meaning." *Nursing Philosophy* 2, pp. 163–176.

Alvesson M. and D. Karreman (2000). "Varieties of Discourse: On the Study of Organizations through Discourse Analysis." *Human Relations* 53(9), pp. 1125–1149.

Alvarez, F. (2001). "Le rôle de la confiance dans l'échange d'information : étude de relations de contrôle en milieu hospitalier." Thèse de Doctorat, Université Paris Dauphine, décembre.

Alvarez, F. (2002). "Building Typologies from Discourse: A Study of Control Relationships in a French Public Hospital." 5th International Conference on Organizational Discourse, London, July.

Alvarez-Pompilius, F. and C. Easley (2003). "Towards a Theoretical Model for Managing Diversity and Culture in Organizations." Proceedings of the Sam/IFSAM VII World Congress, Goteborg, Sweden, 2004.

Anzaldúa, G. (2007). *Borderlands/La Frontera, the New Mestiza*. 3rd edition. San Francisco: Aunt Lute Books.

Anzaldúa, G. and A. Keating (eds.) (2002). *This Bridge We Call Home, Radical Visions for Transformation*. New York: Routledge.

Augustine, A. (2006). Personal interview, May 2, 2006, 8:22 pm.

Barrett, F. and D. Cooperrider (1990). "Generative Metaphor Intervention: A New Approach for Working with Systems Divided by Conflict and Caught in Defensive Perception." *The Journal of Applied Behavioral Science* 26(2), pp. 222–224.

Barrett, F., G. Thomas, and S. Hocevar (1995). "The Central Role of Discourse in Large Scale Change: A Social Construction Perspective." *The Journal of Applied Behavioral Science* 31, pp. 353–372.

Barrett, F. and S. Srivastva (1991). "History as a Mode of Inquiry in Organizational Life: A Role for Human Cosmogony." *Human Relations* 44, pp. 236–244.

Bastein, D., R. McPhee, and K. Bolton (1995). "A Study and Extended Theory of the Structuration of Climate." *Communication Monographs* 62, pp. 87–109.

Bauman, H. (1992). *French Creoles in Louisiana: An American Tale.* http://www.yale.edu/ynhti/curriculum/units/1992/2/92.02.02.x.html.

Beattie, V. and S. Smith (2010). "Human Capital, Value Creation and Disclosure." *Journal of Human Resource Costing and Accounting* 14(4), pp. 262–285.

Bellou, V. (2007). "Shaping Psychological Contracts in the Public and Private Sectors: A Human Resources Management Perspective." *International Public Management Journal* 10(3), pp. 327–349.

Bhawuk, D. and R. Brislin (2000). "Cross-Cultural Training: A Review." *Applied Psychology: An International Reivew* 49(1), pp. 162–191.

Bissett, N. (2004). "Diversity Writ Large: Forging the Link between Diverse People and Diverse Organizational Possibilities." *Journal of Organizational Change Management* 17(3), pp. 315–325.

Bjerregard, T., J. Lauring, and K. Anders (2009). "A Critical Analysis of Intercultural Communication Research in Cross-Cultural Management: Introducing New Developments in Anthropology." *Critical Perspectives on International Business* 5(3), pp. 207–228.

Boesak, A. (2009). *Running with Horses: Reflections of an Accidental Politician.* Cape Town: Joho Publishers.

Bonet, L. and E. Negrier (2011). "The End(s) of National Cultures? Cultural Policy in the Face of Diversity." *International Journal of Cultural Policy* 17(5), pp. 574–589.

Brief, A., R. Buttram, R. Reizenstein, S. Pugh, J. Callahan, R. McCline, and J. Vaslow (1997). "Beyond Good Intentions: The Next Steps toward Racial Equality in the American Workplace." *The Academy of Management Executive* 11(4), Nov. 1997, p. 59.

Brown, M. (2004). *Blackening of the Bible.* New York: Trinity Press International.

The California Board of Regents v. Bakke. http://score.rims.k12.ca.us/score_lessons/evolution_of_civilrights/bakke.htm. Downloaded May 6, 2013.

The California Board of Regents v. Bakke. http://en.wikipedia.org/wiki/Regents_of_the_University_of_California_v._Bakke. Downloaded May 6, 2013.

Cantrell, S., J. Benton, T. Laudal, and R. Thomas (2006). "Measuring the Value of Human Capital Investments: The SAP Case." *Strategy and Leadership* 34(2) pp. 43–52.

Chia R. (2000) "Discourse Analysis as Organizational Analysis." *Organization* 7(3), pp. 513–518.

Claerbaut, D. (1983). *Urban Ministry.* Grand Rapids, MI: Zondervan Publishing House.

Clawson, J. G. (2009). *Level Three Leadership.* New York: Pearson Education.

Cone, J. (1970). *A Black Theology of Liberation.* New York: J. B. Lippincott.

Cooperrider, D. (1986). "Appreciative Inquiry: Toward a Methodology for Understanding and Enhancing Organizational Innovation." Unpublished dissertation, Case Western Reserve University, Cleveland.

Cooperrider, D. L. and S. Srivastva (1987). "Appreciative Inquiry in Organizational Life." In *Research in Organizational Change and Development*. Vol. 1. Edited by R. W. Woodman and W. A. Pasmore, pp. 129–169. Stamford, CT: JAI Press,

Cox T. (1994). *Cultural Diversity in Organizations,* San Francisco, CA: Berrett-Koehler Publishers.

Cox, T. and S. Blake (1991). "Managing Cultural Diversity: Implications for Organizational Competitiveness," *The Executive* 5(3), 45–56.

Cross, E. (2000). *Managing Diversity—the Courage to Lead*. WestPoint, CT: Quorum Books.

Daft, R. L. (2011). *The Leadership Experience*. Mason: South-Western Cengage Learning.

Davies, B. (1991). The Concept of Agency: A Feminist Post-Structuralist Analysis. *Social Analysis* 30, 42–53.

Ditomaso, N. (2013). http://opinionator.blogs.nytimes.com/2013/05/05/how-social-networks-drive-black-unemployment/. Downloaded May 8, 2013.

Dobbin, F., S. Kim, and A. Kalev (2011). "You Can't Always Get What You Need: Organizational Determinants of Diversity Programs." *American Sociological Review* 76(3), pp. 386–411.

du Plessis, A. (2012). "Human Resource's Approach Towards Social Responsibility in a Developing Country in the Future: Some Empirical Evidence." *Interdisciplinary Journal of Contemporary Research in Business* 4(1), pp. 204–212.

Easley, C. A. (2001). "Developing, Valuing and Managing Diversity in the New Millennium." *The Organization Development Journal* 19(4), Winter 2001, pp. 38–50.

Easley, C. A. (2002). "Leading to the Winner's Circle: Appreciative Inquiry … A Viable Component of Diversity Management?" Proceedings of the Midwest Academy of Management, April 2002.

Easley, C. A. (2003). Excerpts from the keynote address titled "Loving and Appreciating Our Families, Youth and Communities as We Define Our Future." The National Black Catholic Congress, *Black Catholic Monthly*, www.nbccongress.org, June 2003.

Easley, C. A. (2010). "Expanding a Conversation: Is How We Live as a Culturally Diverse Society Congruent with Our Underlying Assumptions, Methodologies and Theories Regarding Change?" *Journal of Applied Behavioral Science* 46(1), pp. 55–72.

Easley, C. A (2011). "Developing My Higher Self: My Life as an African American Woman in the Academy." In *The Black Professoriate: Negotiating a Habitable Space in the Academy*. Edited by S. Jackson and R. G. Johnson III. New York: Peter Lang.

Easley, C. A. and F. Alvarez-Pompilius (2003). "Qualitative Investigations: Evoking Change and Egalitarianism in a Knowledge Based World." Academy of Management Conference Proceedings.

Easley, C. A. and F. Alvarez-Pompilius (2003). "A New Paradigm for Qualitative Investigations: Towards an Integrative Model for Evoking Change." *Organization Development Journal* 22(3), Fall 2004.

Easley, C. A. and J. W. Swain (2003). "Niccolo Machiavelli: Moving through the Future as We Learn from the Past." International Journal of Organization Theory and Behavior 6(1), Spring 2003.

Fish, S. (1999). *Doing What Comes Naturally*. Durham, NC: Duke University Press.

Ford, J. (1999). "Organizational Change as Shifting Conversations." *Journal of Organizational Change Management* 12(6), pp. 480–500.

Foucault, M. (1986). "Of Other Spaces." *Diacritics* 16, pp. 22–29.

Freire, P. (2006). *Pedagogy of the Oppressed*. 30th anniversary edition. New York: Continuum Publishing.

Friday, E. and S. Friday (2003). "Managing Diversity Using a Strategic Planned Change Approach." *Journal of Management Development* 22(9/10), p. 862.

Friedman, V. and A. Antal (2005). "Negotiating Reality, a Theory of Action Approach to Intercultural Competence," *Managing Learning* 36(1), March 2005, p. 69086.

Gergen, K, and T. Thatchenkery (1996). "Organization Science as Social Construction: Postmodern Potentials," *Journal of Applied Behavioral Analysis* 32, pp. 356–377.

Gladwin, T. N. (1998). Comments on David C. Korten's "Do Corporations Rule the World? And Does it Matter?" *Organization & Environment* 11(4), December 1998, pp. 402–406.

Golembiewski, R. T. (1989). *Organization Development, Ideas and Issues*. New Brunswick, NJ: Transaction Publishers.

Golembiewski, R. T. (1995). *Managing Diversity in Organizations*. Tuscaloosa: The University of Alabama Press.

Groschl, S. (2011). "Diversity Management Strategies of Global Hotel Groups." *International Journal of Contemporary Hospitality Management* 23(2), pp. 224–240.

Grossman, R. J. (2000). "Is Diversity Working?" *HR Magazine* 45(3), pp. 46–50.

Hansen, H. (2006). "The Ethno Narrative Approach." *Human Relations* 59(8), pp. 1049–1076.

Harman, W. and J. Hormann (1990). *Creative Work: The Constructive Role of Business in a Transforming Society*. Indianapolis, IN: Knowledge Systems.

Hayles, R. and A. Russell (1997). *The Diversity Directive: Why Some Initiatives Fail and What to Do about It*. New York: McGraw-Hill.

Healy, G. and F. Oikelome (2007). "Equality and Diversity Actors: A Challenge to Traditional Industrial Relations?" *Equal Opportunities International* 26(1), pp. 44–65.

Hearns N., F. Devine, F. Baum (2007). "The Implications of Contemporary Cultural Diversity for the Hospitality Curriculum." *Education & Training* 49(5), pp. 350–363.

Heron, J. (1971). "Experience and Method: An Inquiry into the Concept of Experiential Research." Human Potential Research Project. University of Surrey.

hooks, b. (1995), "Feminism: Crying for Our Souls." *Women & Therapy* 1(1–2), pp. 265–275.

Hopkins, D. N. (2005). *Black Theology of Liberation*. New York: Orbit.

Hopkins, N. and S. Reicher (1997). Social Movement Rhetoric and the Social Psychology of Collective Action: A Case Study of Anti-abortion Mobilization. *Human Relations* 50, pp. 261–286.

Jeffery, P. (1993). "Targeted for Death: Brazil's Street Children." *The Christian Century* 110, Jan. 1993, pp. 52–55.

Jimenez-Cook, S. and B. Kleiner (2005). "Nursing at the Crossroads: Increasing Workforce Diversity and Addressing Health Disparities," *Equal Opportunities International* 24(7/8), pp. 1–10.

Johnston, W. B. and A. E. Packer (1987). *Workforce 2000*. New York: The Hudson Institute.

Karlberg, M. (2005). "The Power of Discourse and the Discourse of Power: Pursuing Peace through Discourse Intervention." *International Journal of Peace Studies* 10(1), Spring/Summer 2005.

Kets de Vries, M. and D. Miller (1987). "Interpreting Organizational Texts." *Journal of Management Studies* 12, pp. 251–273.

Kezar, A., P. Eckel, M. Contreras-McGavin, and J. Stephen (2007). "Creating a Web of Support: An Important Leadership Strategy for Advancing Campus Diversity." *Higher Education* 55, pp. 69–72.

Korten, D. C. (2001). *When Corporations Rule the World*. 2nd edition. Sterling, VA: Kumarian Press and San Francisco: Berrett-Koehler.

Kravitz, D. A. (2002). "Promoting Diversity and Social Justice: Educating People from Privileged Groups." *Personnel Psychology* 55(2), Summer 2002, pp. 507–511.

Loden, M. (1996). *Implementing Diversity*. Chicago: Irwin Professional Publishing.

Ludema, J. (1996). "Narrative Inquiry: Collective Storytelling as a Source of Hope, Knowledge and Action in Organizational Life." Unpublished dissertation, Case Western Reserve University.

Ludema, J., T. Wilmont, and S. Srivastva (1997). "Organizational Hope, Reaffirming the Constructive Task of Social and Organizational Inquiry." *Human Relations* 50(8).

Manning P. K. (1979). "Metaphors of the Field: Varieties of Organizational Discourse." *Administrative Science Quarterly* 24, Dec. 1979, pp. 660–671.

Marcel, G. (1963). *The Existential Background of Human Dignity*. Cambridge, MA: Harvard University Press.

Marques, J. (2008). "Toward Higher Consciousness: A Time for 'US'." *Interbeing* 2(1), Spring 2008, pp. 33–41.

Marshak, R. and D. Grant (2008). "Transforming Talk: The Interplay of Discourse, Power and Change." *Organization Development Journal* 26(3), pp. 33–40.

Maslach, C. and M. Leiter (1997). *The Truth about Burnout.* San Francisco: Jossey Bass.

Maxwell, G. A. (2004). "Minority Report: Taking the Initiative in Managing Diversity at BBC Scotland." *Employee Relations* 26(2), pp. 182–202.

Mclintock, B. (2001). "Trade as If Children Mattered." *International Journal of Social Economics* 28(10–12), pp. 899–910.

Mitchem, S. (2002). *Womanist Theology.* New York: Orbis.

Mohamed, A. A., J. Wisnieki, M. Askar, and I. Syed (2004). "Towards a Theory of Spirituality in the Workplace." *Competitiveness Review* 14(1and 2), pp. 102–107.

Moltmann, J. (2006). *The Politics of Discipleship and Discipleship in Politics.* Oregon: Wipf & Stock.

Moore, R. L. (2003). *Facing the Dragon: Confronting Personal and Spiritual Grandiosity.* Wilmette: Chiron Publications.

Morley, M. and J. Cerdin (2010). "Intercultural Competence in the International Business Arena." *Journal of Managerial Psychology* 25(8), pp. 805–809.

Muhtada, D. (2012). "Managing Workforce Diversity: An Islamic Perspective." *Indonesian Journal of Islam and Muslim Societies* 2(1), June 2012, pp. 79–108.

Negy, C. and Eisenman, R. (2005). "A Comparison of Afrcan American and White College Students' Affective and Attitudinal Reactions to Lesbians, Gay and Bisexual Individuals: An Exploratory Study." *The Journal of Sex Research* 42(4), 291–298.

Neuert, J., A. Open, and D. Schaupp (2002). "Intercultural Perceptions of Business and Management Practices: A German-American Learning Experience." *Journal of American Academy of Business* 1(2), March 2002, pp. 385–388.

Nichols, Martha (1994). "Does New Age Business Have a Message for Managers?" *Harvard Business Review* 72(2), March/Apr. 1994, pp. 52–54.

Oakes L. S., B. Townley, and D. J. Cooper (1998), "Business Planning as Pedagogy: Language and Control in a Changing Institutional Field." *Administrative Science Quarterly* 43, June 1998, pp. 257–292.

Okoro, E, and M. Washington (2012). "Workforce Diversity and Organizational Communication: Analysis of Human Capital Performance and Productivity." *Journal of Diversity Management* 7(1), pp. 57–62.

Oswick, C., T. Keenoy, and D. Grant (2000). "Discourse, Organizations and Organizing: Concepts, Objects and Subjects." *Human Relations* 53(9), pp. 1115–1120.

Oyler, J. D. and M. G. Pryor (2009). "Workplace Diversity in the United States: The Perspective of Peter Drucker." *Journal of Management History* 15(4), pp. 420–451.

Ozen, S. and F. Kusku (2009). "Corporate Environmental Citizenship Variation in Developing Countries: An Institutional Framework." *Journal of Business Ethics* 89, pp. 297–313.

Ozgener, S. (2008). "Diversity Management and Demographic Differences–Based Discrimination: The Case of Turkish Manufacturing Industry." *Journal of Business Ethics* 82, pp. 621–631.

Parry, J. (2003). "Making Sense of Executive Sensemaking." *Journal of Organization and Management* 17(4), pp. 240–263.

Paskoff, S. (1996). "Ending the Workplace Diversity Wars," *Training* 33(8), Aug. 1996, pp. 42–47.

Perry, S. (2005). New Orleans: Survivor Stories. http://www.citypages.com/databank/26/1294/article13694.asp.

Pettigrew, A. M. (1979). "On Studying Organizational Cultures." *Administrative Science Quarterly* 24, pp. 570–581.

Polanyi, M. (1967). *The Tacit Dimension*. London: Routledge/Kegan Paul.

Quinn, R. E. (1996). *Deep Change: Discovering the Leader within*. San Francisco: Jossey-Bass.

Quinn, R. E. (2000). *Change the World, How Ordinary People Can Accomplish Extraordinary Results*. San Francisco: Jossey Bass.

Quinn, R. E. (2004). *Building the Bridge as You Walk on It*. San Francisco: Jossey Bass.

Quinn, R. E., G. M. Spreitzer, and M. V. Brown (2000). "Changing Others through Changing Ourselves: The Transformation of Human Systems." *Journal of Management Inquiry* 9(2), pp. 147–164.

Reason, P. (1988). *Human Inquiry in Action, Developments in New Paradigm Research*. Newbury Park, CA: Sage Publications.

Redmond, D. (2006). "The Influence of Knowledge of Homosexuality and Religious Importance to Homophobia among African American Students at a Historically Black College." Unpublished doctoral dissertation, Houston, TX: Texas Southern University.

Reynolds, L. and L. Powell (1981). "Black Lesbian Bibliography." *Off Our Backs* 11(9), pp. 9–17.

Robinson-Easley, C. A. (2010)."Easing Our Path: The Healing Power of Dialogue for African American Women in Leadership." In *Women of Color: Taking Their Rightful Place in Leadership*, Edited by Richard G. Johnson III and G. L. A. Harris. San Diego: Birkdale Publishers.

Robinson-Easley, C. A. (2012). *Our Children, Our Responsibilities: Saving the Youth We Are Losing to Gangs*. New York: Peter Lang.

Robinson-Easley, C. A. (2013). *From the Lens of Color: Preparing for Today's Global Workforce*. New York: Palgrave Macmillan.

Rynes,S. and B. Rosen (1995). "A Field Survey of Factors Affecting the Adoption and Perceived Success of Diversity Training." *Personnel Psychology* A8(2), Summer 1995, pp. 247–270.

Schein E. H. (1992). *Organizational Culture and Leadership*. San Francisco: Jossey-Bass Publishers.

Seymen, O. (2006). "The Cultural Diversity Phenomenon Organisations and Different Approaches for Effective Cultural Diversity Management: A Literary Review." *Cross Cultural Management: An International Journal* 13(4).

Singer, J. (1994). *Boundaries of the Soul: The Practice of Jung's Psychology*. New York: Anchor Books.

Styhre, A. and U. Eriksson-Zetterquist (2008). "Thinking the Multiple in Gender and Diversity Studies: Examining the Concept of Intersectionality." *Gender in Management: An International Journal* 23(8), pp. 567–582.

Swain, J. W. (1997). "Niccolo Machiavelli and Modern Public Administration." In *Handbook of Organization Theory and Management: The Philosophical Approach*. Edited by Todd J. Dicker and Thomas D. Lynch, pp.71–95. New York: Marcel Dekker.

Syed, J. and R. Kramar (2010). "What Is the Australian Model for Managing Cultural Diversity?" *Personnel Review* 39(1), pp. 96–115.

Tatli, A. and M. Ozbligin (2009). "Understanding Diversity Managers' Role in Organizational Change: Towards a Conceptual Framework." *Canadian Journal of Administrative Sciences* 26(3), pp. 244–258.

Tenkasi, R., T. Thatchenkery, F. Barrett, and M. Manning (1994). "The Impact of Schemas and Inquiry on Consultants' Constructions of Expectations about the Client System." *CEO Publications* (G) 94–13(256), pp. 1–29.

Thatchenkery, T. J. (1992). "Organizations as "Texts": Hermeneutics as a Model for Understanding Organizational Change." In *Research in Organization Change and Development*. Edited by W. A. Pasmore and R. W. Woodman. Vol. 6, pp. 197–233. Greenwich: JAI Press.

Thatchenkery, T. (1996). "Affirmation as Facilitation. A Postmodernist Paradigm in Change Management," *OD Practitioner* 28(1&2).

Thomas, R. (1991). *Beyond Race and Gender*. New York: American Management Association.

Thurman, H. (1963). *Disciplines of the Spirit*. Richmond: Friends United Press.

Triandis, H., Chan, D. Bhawuk, S. Iwao, and J. Sinha (1995). "Multimethod Probes of Allocentrism and Idiocentrism." *International Journal of Psychology* 30(4), pp. 461–480.

Vaill, P. (1996). *Learning as a Way of Being*. San Francisco: Jossey-Bass.

Wang, C. and A. Mattila (2010). "A Grounded Theory Model of Service Providers' Stress, Emotion, and Coping during Intercultural Service Encounters." *Managing Service Quality* 20(4), pp. 328–342.

Watson, B., P. Spoonley, and E. Fitzgerald (2009). "Managing Diversity: A Twenty-First Century Agenda." *New Zealand Journal of Employment Relations (Online)* 34(2).

Westaway, J. (2012). "Globalization, Transnational Corporations and Human Rights—A New Paradigm." *International Law Research* 1(1), pp. 63–72.

"When Death Squads Meet Street Children." (1993) *Economist*, July 1993, p. 39.

White-Zappa, B. (2001). "Hopeful Corporate Citizenship: A Quantitative and Qualitative Examination of the Relationship between Organizational Hope, Appreciative Inquiry, and Organizational Citizenship Behaviors." Unpublished doctoral dissertation, Benedictine University, Lisle, IL.

Wink, W. (1992). *Engaging the Powers: Discernment and Resistance in a World of Domination.* Minneapolis: Fortress Press.

Wulf, C. (2013). "Human Development in a Globalized Word. Education towards Peace, Culture Diversity and Sustainable Development." *Revista Espanola de Pedagogia* 24, pp. 71–86.

Yaeger, T., P. Sorensen, C. Easley (2002). "Readying an Organization for Diversity Challenges." *Training Today.* January/February 2002.

INDEX

Printed and bound by CPI Group (UK) Ltd, Croydon, CR0 4YY